THE ART OF WOODWORKING

CABINETS
AND BOOKCASES

THE ART OF WOODWORKING

CABINETS AND BOOKCASES

TIME-LIFE BOOKS
ALEXANDRIA, VIRGINIA

ST. REMY PRESS
MONTREAL • NEW YORK

THE ART OF WOODWORKING was produced by
ST. REMY PRESS

PUBLISHER	Kenneth Winchester
PRESIDENT	Pierre Léveillé
Series Editor	Pierre Home-Douglas
Series Art Director	Francine Lemieux
Senior Editors	Marc Cassini (Text)
	Heather Mills (Research)
Art Directors	Normand Boudreault, Luc Germain,
	Solange Laberge
Designers	Jean-Guy Doiron, Michel Giguère,
	Hélène Dion
Research Editor	Jim McRae
Picture Editor	Christopher Jackson
Writers	Andrew Jones, Rob Lutes
Research Assistant	Bryan Quinn
Contributing Illustrators	Gilles Beauchemin, Rolland Bergera,
	Michel Blais, Jean-Pierre Bourgeois,
	Ronald Durepos, Robert Paquet,
	James Thérien
Administrator	Natalie Watanabe
Production Manager	Michelle Turbide
System Coordinator	Jean-Luc Roy
Photographer	Robert Chartier
Proofreader	Judith Yelon
Indexer	Christine M. Jacobs

Time-Life Books is a division of Time-Life Inc.,
a wholly owned subsidiary of
THE TIME INC. BOOK COMPANY

TIME-LIFE BOOKS

President	John D. Hall
Vice-President	Nancy K. Jones
Editor-in-Chief	Thomas H. Flaherty
Director of Editorial Resources	Elise D. Ritter-Clough
Marketing Director	Regina Hall
Editorial Director	Lee Hassig
Consulting Editor	John R. Sullivan
Production Manager	Marlene Zack

THE CONSULTANTS

Jon Arno is a consultant, cabinetmaker and freelance writer who lives in Troy, Michigan. He also conducts seminars on wood identification and early American furniture design.

Kam Ghaffari is a freelance writer and editor. He has his own business in Rhode Island designing and building one-of-a-kind and limited production furniture. Kam's background also includes working professionally in furniture reproduction and fine carpentry, and studying with furniture patriarchs Wendell Castle of the U.S. and Fred Baier of England.

Giles Miller-Mead taught advanced cabinetmaking at Montreal technical schools for more than ten years. A native of New Zealand, he has worked as a restorer of antique furniture.

Joseph Truini is Senior Editor of *Home Mechanix* magazine. A former Shop and Tools Editor of *Popular Mechanics*, he has worked as a cabinetmaker, home improvement contractor and carpenter.

Cabinets and bookcases
p. cm.—(The Art of Woodworking)
Includes index.
ISBN 0-8094-9945-2 (trade)
1. Cabinetwork—Amateurs' manuals.
2. Bookcases—Amateurs' manuals.
I. Time-Life Books. II. Series
TT197.C23
684.1'6—dc20   93-20771
                                      CIP

For information about any Time-Life book,
please call 1-800-621-7026, or write:
Reader Information
Time-Life Customer Service
P.O. Box C-32068
Richmond, Virginia
23261-2068

CONTENTS

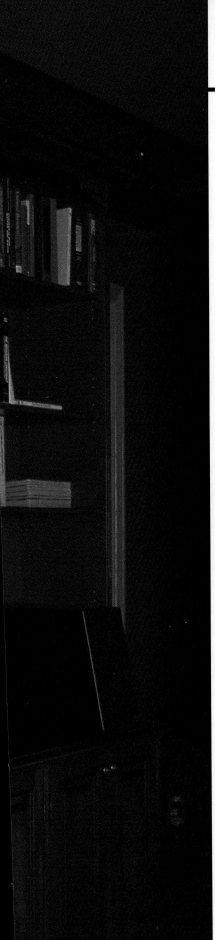

Alain Morcel and his
LIBRARY UNIT

The library unit shown here, made out of Honduras mahogany, was one of my first big commissions. It was built in the shop I co-own with Frédéric Loeven, a fine cabinetmaker. We had built a lot of single pieces in the past, but this was our first opportunity to experiment with the planning and construction of a large, integrated wall unit.

Our first step was to take accurate measurements of the room that the unit would occupy. This had to be done very carefully, since walls are not always straight. The difference can be as much as ¾ inch. So we measured between the walls at the corners of the room and again every few inches out. We only wanted to cut our stock once!

With measurements in hand, we designed the piece in the shop. Our client wanted a traditional English-library look, which was why we chose a dark mahogany. The French doors also contributed to the classical appearance of the unit.

The most critical design consideration was to make sure the bookcases would be well proportioned for the size of the room. The relationship between the height, depth and width of the unit had to be right. To provide ourselves with a visual reference as we cut and assembled the components of the structure, we drew a full-scale plan of the room on the floor of the shop. This enabled us to keep track of all the pieces and position them in their proper locations as we went along.

We used mahogany-veneered fiberboard for the basic structure and joined the pieces with biscuits. Most of the shelves are adjustable; they sit on brass shelf supports which are screwed into sleeves in the side panels. We added solid mahogany banding, twice the thickness of the shelf stock, to the front edges of the shelves to give them more rigidity. The back panels sit in rabbets cut into the back edges of the unit. We made the paneled doors out of solid mahogany using mortise-and-tenon joints with a fine integrated molding. The cornice molding is made up of three separate pieces of wood individually shaped and glued together before being applied to the unit.

We finished the bookcases with a dark red mahogany stain followed by several coats of cellulose-based lacquer, then wiped on a glazing stain to accentuate the molding and give the piece an aged appearance.

Alain Morcel operates Les Réalisations Loeven-Morcel, a cabinetry shop in Montréal, Québec, along with his partner, Frédéric Loeven. The shop specializes in architectural woodwork and reproductions of antique furniture.

Chris Becksvoort describes the
CHALLENGES OF CABINETMAKING

Case pieces—cupboards, bureaus, bookcases, chests, sideboards, and other assorted cabinets—are at best merely glorified boxes. Yet there is something special about them. All contain an element of mystery, just waiting to be explored. Who can resist opening a small door with a tiny turned knob and spinner, or lifting the lid of a dovetailed keepsake box? Ask Pandora.

To the cabinetmaker, case pieces are a pleasure, as well as a challenge to build. The possible layout combinations are endless: doors, drawers, shelves, pull-out trays, dividers, pigeonholes, and one of my favorite components, secret compartments. Nothing thrills a customer more than to be told that their new acquisition has a hidden compartment. And nothing adds to the anticipation more than to say it is up to them to find it.

Woodworkers specializing in individually built pieces thrive on variety. I concentrate on cases that are not available commercially, such as a special-size piece to fit a specific spot, a 15-drawer camera cabinet, a display case for a watch collection, or a tinware cupboard like the one shown in the photograph. It was inspired by a Shaker original I saw at the Renwick Gallery of the Smithsonian Institution in 1973. The cupboard is one of the most versatile pieces I build, equally suitable in a hallway, bedroom, bath, kitchen, or living room—anywhere space is at a premium.

Each piece I make involves the integration of function and design. The real challenge comes in the building process. Wood expands during summer's humidity and shrinks during winter's dryness. A board moves across its width, while its length remains virtually constant. Any constraint that physically limits this movement invites disaster. Moldings cannot be glued across a cabinet side; instead they ride on dovetails. Door frames are cut from relatively narrow quartersawn wood to minimize movement, while the wide panels are free to float in their grooves. The frames between drawers must telescope in and out of their mortise-and-tenon joints to follow the movement of the case sides. Backs, like doors, consist of quartersawn frames and floating panels, mortised and tenoned to provide strength and resist racking. Even the gaps above each drawer must be figured precisely to keep them from swelling shut.

When the elements of design, wood, and joinery come together correctly, the case will survive so that future generations will become intrigued enough to want to turn the knob, open the door, and search for the secret compartment.

Chris Becksvoort builds fine furniture at his workshop in New Gloucester, Maine. He is shown here with his tinware cupboard in the Meeting House at the Shaker community of Sabbathday Lake, Maine.

Mario Rodriguez talks about building his

CORNER CUPBOARD

When my wife and I started house-hunting in the country we looked at new contemporary homes, new houses built in traditional styles, and old houses. Naturally, we considered things like layout, heating systems, and dependable plumbing. But we were still drawn to old houses. For me, there was the knowledge that an old house was built by hand—from the hand-dug foundation right up to the hand-split shingle roof. Old houses were built with sheer strength guided by experience and skill.

We ended up buying an old house.

Walking through our place you see surfaces that undulate and ripple from hand planes that passed over them nearly 200 years ago. There are chestnut beams with shimmering, faceted surfaces cut by an adze and thick, pine floorboards studded with hand-wrought nails. All the doorways, mantels, and paneling were produced with hand planes from choice Hudson Valley pine. No flakeboard or finger-jointed base molding here.

I wanted to build a special piece for the dining room. With its massive stone fireplace, it is the heart of the house. In the 18th Century, life revolved around this room. I decided to build the corner cupboard shown in the photo and place it opposite the fireplace. It's likely that a similar piece occupied the same spot many years ago.

I built the cupboard from tiger maple; much of it was made using antique hand tools. I shaped the molding with planes and scrapers, some of which I made myself. The hard maple surfaces were hand planed, not sanded, and up close you can see small bits of tearout—just as you would find on cupboards from the 18th Century. The interior of the case is fairly straightforward, aside from a few angles. It is made of pine and joined with dadoes and rabbet joints secured with small cut nails. I mortised and tenoned the cabinet frames and fitted the sash with old, seeded glass. I even used a dark, less-refined shellac to give the wood a warm honey color. Then it was rubbed with a mixture of pumice and linseed oil to achieve an antique-like satin finish. I made the cabinet as it would have been built 200 years ago. When it was completed and placed in the corner, the cupboard and the room came to life. Together they take you back to the 18th Century. It's a perfect match.

Like a painting, a piece of furniture needs the proper setting to create the right mood and atmosphere. Not only is the proper period environment important, but so is scale, color, and lighting. These are considerations that will heighten the impact of the piece and contribute to its success. I would enjoy my cupboard planted anywhere but without a doubt I enjoy it *more* in the dining room of my beautiful old home.

Mario Rodriguez teaches woodworking at Warwick Country Workshops in Warwick, New York, and at the Fashion Institute of Technology in New York City. He is also a contributing editor of Fine Woodworking *magazine.*

CABINETMAKING BASICS

Panels are often made of boards edge-glued together. The pieces should produce a pattern that is visually interesting, while the grain of all the boards should run in the same direction. A marked triangle will help you rearrange the boards correctly if they are moved before glue up.

There are two kinds of skill involved in constructing a fine cabinet or bookcase: putting together the basic skeleton of the piece and then embellishing it. The finials and rosettes of the Queen Anne highboy featured on page 106 must be turned with care on a lathe and then artfully carved; the distinctive pilasters of an armoire *(page 60)* require careful attention to produce on the router. But although these distinctive adornments may capture a viewer's attention, they also reflect a truism: No amount of decoration will conceal the defects of a poorly built structure. This chapter looks in detail at the basic skills you will need to select stock, prepare it professionally, and then assemble it into a sturdy foundation for your cabinet or bookcase.

The basics of cabinetmaking begin with an understanding of wood. The sections on dealing with wood movement *(page 14)*, ordering wood *(page 16)*, and preparing a cutting list based on a sketch *(page 18)* will help you purchase the right lumber for your project.

With your stock in hand, you can begin the step-by-step process of building a carcase. This begins with preparing stock *(page 20)* and gluing up panels *(page 24)*. A variety of corner joinery options, including hand-cut dovetails and plate (or biscuit) joints, are presented beginning on page 26. Next comes installing a back panel *(page 31)* and final glue-up and assembly.

The frame-and-panel method of building a cabinet is described starting on page 32. This technique is popular not only for its appearance, but because it allows for wood movement. In many frame-and-panel cabinets, the panels are "raised"—that is, they have bevels cut around their edges. Not only do the bevels lend a decorative touch, but they also allow the wood to expand and contract while preserving the work's integrity. Raising panels is shown starting on page 36.

A skew chisel removes slivers of waste from the dovetails in a drawer side. Cutting the joint by hand is painstaking, but it imparts a traditional and distinctive look to a piece of furniture.

WOOD MOVEMENT

Wood is a hygroscopic material, absorbing and releasing moisture as the relative humidity of the surrounding air rises and falls. And as the moisture content of a piece of wood changes, so do its dimensions and weight. When wood is assembled into a piece of furniture, the changes can produce problems—some great, some small. A cabinet door that shuts smoothly in December may not close at all in June; a perfectly square bookcase can literally pull itself apart at the joints as humidity changes throughout the year. Knowing how moisture affects wood will help you avoid these problems.

The water in wood is measured as a percentage of its oven-dry, or water-free weight. For example, if a 40-pound piece of wood drops to 30 pounds when oven-dried, the weight of the shed water—10 pounds—divided by the wood's dry weight—30 pounds—is the moisture content of the original piece: in this case, 33 percent.

Wood holds water both as vapor-like moisture called free water in its cell cavities and as bound water in the cell walls. When wood is cut and exposed to the air, it sheds its free water first. When all free water is expelled, the wood is said to be at its fiber saturation point (FSP), typically between 23 and 30 percent moisture content. To this point there has been no change in the dimensions of the piece; it simply weighs less. As wood dries further, however, water is shed from the cell walls, causing them—and the board—to shrink.

Under normal circumstances, wood never regains its free water; a dried board's cell cavities will always remain empty of moisture. But the amount of bound water contained in the cell walls changes with shifts in the humidity in the air. At 100 percent relative humidity, wood reaches its FSP. At 0 percent humidity, wood is drained of all water. The relative moisture in the atmosphere normally falls between these values, and the moisture content of most woods ranges between 5 and 20 percent. Still, the fluctuation in relative humidity between typical North American winters and summers can cause substantial wood movement over the course of a year.

You can compensate for this in several ways. Use a humidifier in winter and a dehumidifier in summer to keep the indoor level of humidity as constant as possible. Remember to make allowances for wood movement in the construction of your work. Using frame-and-panel joinery for example *(page 32)* will provide space for wood to expand and contract without affecting the overall condition of the piece. Some woods tend to move more than others; consult a lumber dealer to find the most dimensionally stable species for your projects.

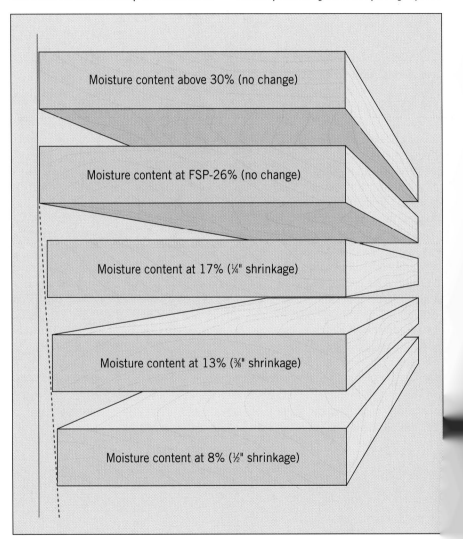

Moisture content above 30% (no change)

Moisture content at FSP-26% (no change)

Moisture content at 17% (¼" shrinkage)

Moisture content at 13% (⅜" shrinkage)

Moisture content at 8% (½" shrinkage)

As the moisture level of a 2-by-10 plain-sawn plank of softwood lumber drops below the fiber saturation point (FSP), the wood shrinks. At 17 percent, the board is ¼ inch narrower than it was at its FSP; it loses another ¼ inch of width when kiln-dried to 8 percent. Shrinkage depends partly on the density of the wood; generally, a denser species shrinks and swells more than a lighter one. Sapwood also tends to change in size more quickly than heartwood.

WOOD SHRINKAGE

Tangential and radial shrinkage

Wood does not shrink uniformly; as shown by the dotted red lines in the illustration at right, tangential shrinkage—tangent to the growth rings—is about twice as great as radial shrinkage, which occurs across the rings. This difference causes boards and panels to warp as they shrink or swell with changes in relative humidity. It can also cause joints to loosen or tighten from excess pressure, as discussed below. Shrinkage along the length of a board is usually insignificant. A 2-by-10 plank that shrinks ½ inch across its width might lose less than 1/16 inch along an 8-foot length.

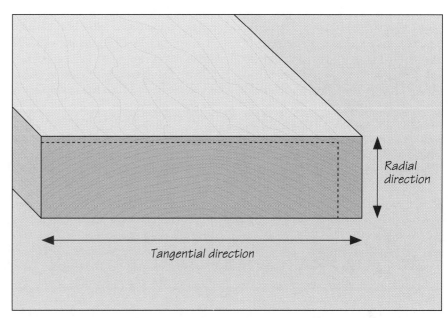

Radial direction

Tangential direction

WOOD GRAIN AND JOINERY

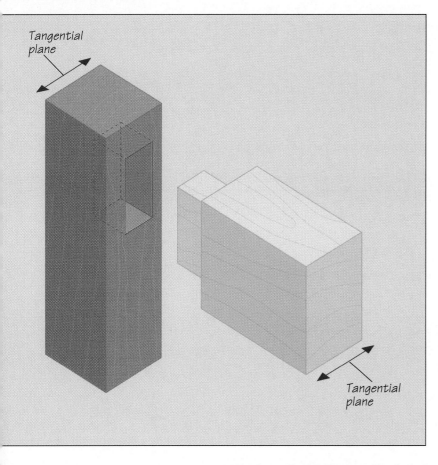

Tangential plane

Tangential plane

Optimizing grain direction

The location of the tangential planes of mating boards will significantly affect a joint's strength and stability. In the ideal situation—as shown in the illustration of a mortise-and-tenon joint at left—the tangential planes of joined pieces are parallel. This ensures that the boards will experience similar wood movement in the same direction as their moisture content changes. Orienting boards this way helps prevent a joint from coming loose; it also prevents the mating boards from splitting when they swell with higher levels of moisture.

SELECTING AND ORDERING LUMBER

You can buy the lumber for your woodworking project from several sources, each with its own advantages and drawbacks. The local lumberyard is often the most convenient supplier, but the selection may be limited to construction woods such as pine, spruce, and other softwoods. Though you may find the occasional cache of hardwood at a lumberyard, you will probably have to venture farther afield, consulting woodworking magazines to find dealers who specialize in the hardwoods used in cabinetry. Prices for good hardwood lumber can be high, but as is often the case, you will generally get what you pay for.

Sometimes you can buy locally cut lumber from a small sawmill, but the wood will often need to be seasoned and surfaced. Recycled boards are growing in popularity, a result of the scarcity of certain woods and the growing sense of environmental responsibility felt by many woodworkers. Whether removed from an old barn or a piece of timeworn furniture, such wood may be relatively inexpensive and, because it often originates from old growth timber, it can be visually and structurally superior to the small billets of younger lumber available today.

Before ordering your wood, consider your requirements carefully and refer to the following tips to help you get what you need at a reasonable cost.

• **Species:** Ask for the specific wood species, not a broad family name. For example, order Western red cedar, n simply cedar. To be absolutely sure, lea the botanical name of the wood yc want and ask for it.

• **Quantity:** Let your supplier kno whether you are ordering in board fe or lineal feet. A lineal foot refers to board's length, regardless of its wid and thickness. The board foot is a mea sure of the volume of wood; it is usua ly necessary to refer to board feet fc ordering hardwoods, which are ofte available in random sizes only.

• **Size:** Wood is sold in nominal rath than actual sizes, so make allowances fc the difference when ordering surfacc lumber. A nominal 2-by-4 is actual 1½"-by-3½". The thickness of wood often expressed as a fraction in quarte

---

CALCULATING BOARD FEET

Ordering lumber by the board foot

The board foot is a unit of measurement commonly used when dealing with hardwood lumber. As shown below, the standard board foot is equivalent to a piece of wood 1 inch thick, 12 inches wide, and 12 inches long. To calculate the number of board feet in a particular piece of wood, multiply its three dimensions, then divide the result by 144 if the dimensions are all in inches, or by 12 if one of the dimensions is in feet.

The formula for a standard board:
1" x 12" x 12" ÷ 144 = 1 (or 1" x 12" x 1' ÷ 12 = 1)
So if you had a 6-foot-long 1-by-4, you would calculate the board feet as follows: 1" x 4" x 6' ÷ 12 = 2 (or 2 board feet). Other examples are shown in the illustration. Remember that board feet are calculated on the basis of nominal rather than actual dimensions.

*Number of board feet
in eight lineal feet of
different size boards*

1-by-3 = 2 board feet

1-by-6 = 4 board feet

1-by-12 = 8 board feet

2-by-4 = 5 ⅓ board feet

2-by-6 = 8 board feet

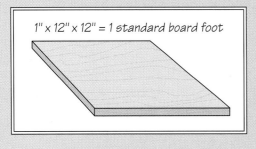

1" x 12" x 12" = 1 standard board foot

an inch. A 2-inch-thick board, for example, is expressed as ⁸⁄₄; surfacing will reduce it to 1¾ inches. With unsurfaced green wood, the nominal and actual dimensions are the same.

•**Grade:** The primary difference between high and low grades of hardwood lumber is appearance rather than strength. Because the grade of a board is determined by the proportions of clear wood it contains, large high-grade boards are far more expensive than low-grade boards. If you need only small high-grade pieces you can cut them out of a lower-grade board, at great savings. Consult your local dealer for a chart of the different grades available.

•**Seasoning:** Lumber is sold either kiln-dried (KD) or air-dried (AD). The primary difference between the two is the moisture content (MC) of the wood. Kiln-dried wood has a moisture content of about 8 percent; it will not dry any further when used for indoor furniture. Air-dried wood has an MC of 12 to 15 percent. This wood is often chosen by carvers, or by woodworkers who prefer to dry their own wood.

•**Surfacing:** Surfacing refers to how wood is prepared at the mill before it comes to the lumberyard. Hardwood lumber is usually surfaced on both faces (S2S). If you have a planer and a jointer, buying rough lumber and surfacing it yourself will prove less expensive.

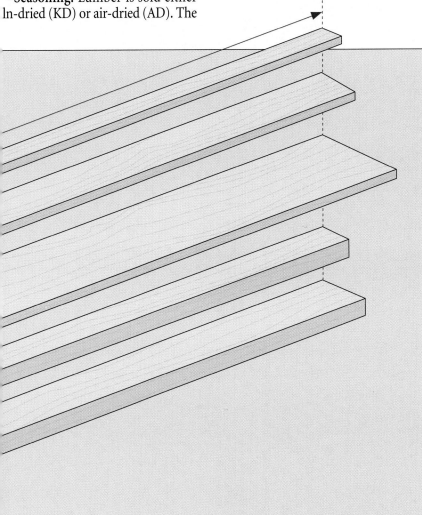

THE STAGES OF CABINET PRODUCTION

Like most tasks, the building of a piece of furniture can be accomplished most smoothly and efficiently if you take a methodical approach. Most projects involve the steps listed below; they should be carried out in the sequence shown, starting at the drawing board and ending with a final inspection. For maximum efficiency, lay out your tools in the shop so that your wood follows a relatively direct route from rough stock to final assembly. Considerations for determining your needs and ordering wood are discussed at left and on page 18. Stock preparation and joinery begin on page 20.

- •Design and plan piece
- •List and order materials
- •Prepare stock
- •Joint one face and edge
- •Plane other face
- •Rip to width
- •Crosscut to length
- •Cut joints
- •Sand before assembly
- •Assemble components
- •Finish sand
- •Make and install doors and drawers
- •Apply finish
- •Give final inspection

CUTTING LISTS

Making and using a cutting list

A cutting list records the finished sizes of lumber needed for a particular piece of furniture. If one is not included with the plans you purchase, you will have to make your own based on a sketch of the design. Use the formula shown on page 16 to total the number of board feet for each component of the project; add 20 to 40 percent (depending on the species) to account for waste and defects in the wood. For the bookcase shown at right, which totals roughly 14 board feet, you should purchase 17 to 20 board feet of ¾ lumber in addition to the plywood for the back of the case. As shown below, a cutting list should include the name of the component, the quantity, the dimensions of each piece, and the wood species selected for the project. For convenience, assign each piece a key letter for later reference.

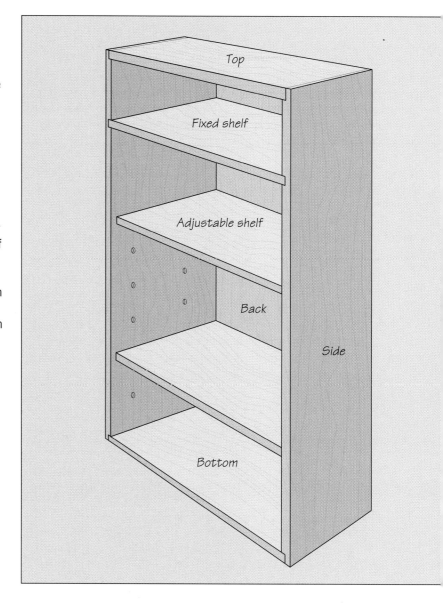

CUTTING LIST

Piece	Qty.	Th.	W.	L.	Material	Board feet
A Top	1	1"	10"	23¼"	ash	1.6
B Bottom	1	1"	10"	23¼"	ash	1.6
C Side	2	1"	10"	42"	ash	5.8
D Fixed shelf	1	1"	10"	23¼"	ash	1.6
E Adjustable shelves	2	1"	10"	22⅜"	ash	3.0
F Back	1	¼"	24"	42"	plywood	—

LUMBER DEFECTS

Lumber defects may reduce a board's strength or workability or mar its appearance. Or, in the hands of a creative woodworker, some defects may in fact become visual assets, transforming an ordinary piece into a work of art.

Most defects, however, are undiminished trouble. Although some may result from damage to the standing tree or the lumber cut from it, the greatest number of defects are produced by irregular drying of the wood.

The chart below illustrates some of the most common defects and details the way in which most can be corrected; with diligent use of the band saw, even the most seriously cupped boards can be salvaged (page 21).

DEFECTS IN WOOD

TYPE	CHARACTERISTICS	REMEDIES
Knot	Appears as a whorl encircled by sound tissue. Formed as girth of tree increases, gradually enveloping branch. Live branches integrate with surrounding wood, resulting in tight knots; dead stubs cannot integrate with surrounding tissue, forming dead or loose knots.	Tight knots can be cut out or used, as appearance dictates; dead or loose knots must be removed before working with stock.
Gum	An accumulation on the surface of the board or in pockets within the board. Usually develops when a tree has suffered an injury, exposure to fire, or insect attack.	Do not use stock if a quality finish is required, as gum will bleed through most finishes.
Checks	Lengthwise ruptures or separations in the wood, usually caused by rapid drying. May compromise strength and appearance of board.	Can be cut off.
Bow	An end-to-end curve along the face, usually caused by improper storage of lumber. Introduces internal stresses in the wood that make it difficult to cut.	Flatten bowed boards on the jointer, or cut into shorter pieces, then use the jointer.
Cup	An edge-to-edge curve across the face. Common in tangentially cut stock, or boards cut close to the pith, if one face of a board has less contact with the air than the other.	Cupped boards can be salvaged on the band saw (page 21) or flattened on the jointer.
Crook	End-to-end curve along the edge, caused by incorrect seasoning or cutting the board close to the pith of a tree. Weakens the wood, making it unsuitable for weight-bearing applications.	Board can be salvaged by jointing and ripping waste from the edges. Crooked boards remain unstable, and may not stain or finish well.
Twist	Uneven or irregular warping when one corner is not aligned with the others. Results from uneven drying or a cross-grain pattern that is not parallel to the edge.	Board can be flattened on jointer, or cut into shorter boards.
Split	Similar to checks, appearing as separations along the growth rings. Also known as ring check or ring shank. Results from improper drying of wood or felling damage.	Board can be used, but split may mar the appearance of the wood, becoming more noticeable when stain is applied.

PREPARING STOCK

Once you have designed a project and purchased the lumber, you must prepare the stock, jointing and planing it smooth and square, cutting it to the proper dimensions and sanding any surfaces that will be difficult to reach when the work is assembled.

The procedures you follow depend on how the wood was surfaced before you bought it. For rough, unsurfaced lumber, first smooth one face on the jointer, then one edge, producing two adjoining surfaces that are at 90° to each other. Next, plane the other face of the board to make it parallel to the first. When the stock is square and smooth, you are ready to rip it to width and crosscut it to length.

For S2S lumber, which has already had both faces surfaced, you need only joint one edge across the jointer, then cut to width and length. S4S stock, with all four surfaces dressed, can be ripped and crosscut immediately; only surfaces that will be glued together must be jointed. Before gluing up any part of your project, remember to sand any surfaces that will be hard to reach after assembly.

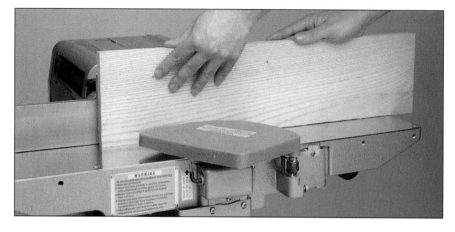

A jointer produces a smooth, even edge on a hardwood board. For best results, set a cutting depth between $1/16$ and $1/8$ inch.

SURFACING LUMBER

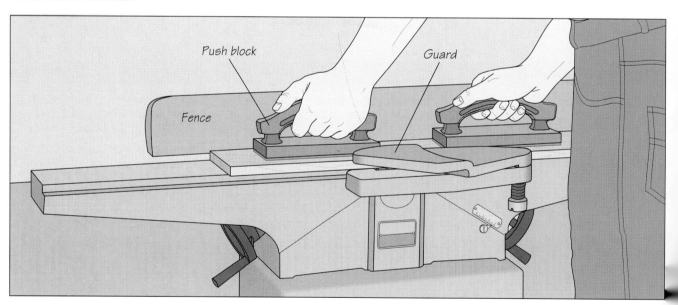

Push block

Guard

Fence

Jointing a board

Slide the fence toward the guard, if necessary, to ensure that no portion of the cutter knives will be exposed as the workpiece passes over them. Lay the workpiece face-down on the infeed table a few inches from the knives. Butt its edge against the fence, then place two push blocks squarely on its face, centered between the edges. (Use push blocks with offset handles to prevent your hands from hitting the fence.) Feed the board slowly and steadily across the knives *(above)* applying downward pressure on the outfeed side of the knives and lateral pressure against the fence. When working with long stock, bring your left hand to the back of the workpiece when your right hand passes the knives. When one face is done, joint the board edge as shown in the photo above.

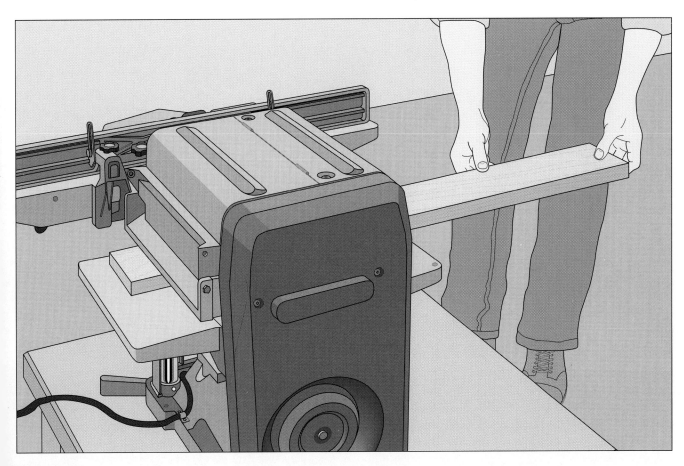

Planing stock

Set the cutting depth to $\frac{1}{16}$ inch. Stand to one side of the planer and use both hands to feed the stock carefully into the machine. Once the feed mechanism grips the board and begins to pull it across the cutterhead, support the trailing end to keep it flat on the table *(above)*. Then move to the outfeed side of the planer to support the workpiece with both hands until it clears the outfeed roller. To prevent the stock from warping in use, avoid planing only one face; instead, plane the same amount of wood from both sides.

SHOP TIP

Salvaging cupped stock on the band saw

You can salvage cupped boards using the band saw, radial arm saw, or table saw by ripping the stock into narrower boards. If you are using the band saw as shown here, install your widest blade and a rip fence. The narrower the width of cut, the flatter the resulting boards. Set the board convex (high) side up on the table and, butting the board against the fence, feed it steadily into the blade. Finish the pass with a push stick. Remove any remaining high spots on the jointer.

DIMENSIONING STOCK

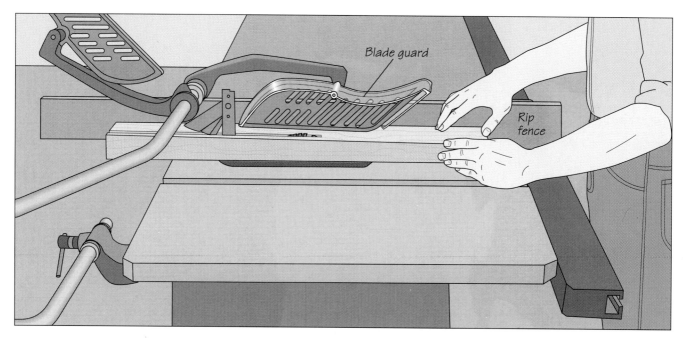

Ripping a board on the table saw

Set the blade height about ¼ inch above the workpiece. Position the rip fence for the width of cut, then push the stock into the blade, holding it firmly against the fence with your left hand and feeding the board with both thumbs *(above)*. Stand slightly to one side of the workpiece and straddle the fence with your right hand, making certain that neither hand is in line with the blade. Keep pushing the board until the blade cuts through it completely. To keep your fingers from coming closer than 3 inches from the blade, use a push stick to complete the pass. **(Caution: Blade guard partially retracted for clarity.)**

Crosscutting stock

With the workpiece flush against the miter gauge, align the cutting mark with the blade. Position the rip fence well away from the end of the stock to prevent the cut-off piece from jamming against the blade and kicking back toward you. Hook the thumbs of both hands over the miter gauge to hold the stock firmly against the gauge and flat on the table, then feed the board into the blade *(right)*. **(Caution: Blade guard partially retracted for clarity.)**

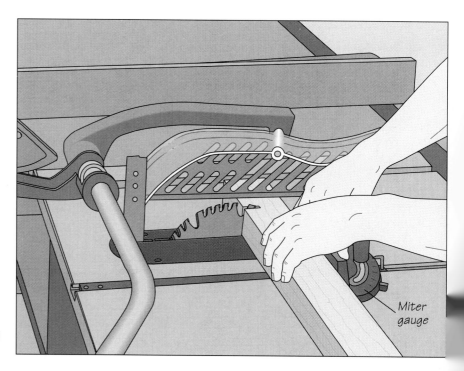

ANDING

Using a belt sander

Clamp a stop block to a work surface to keep the stock from moving. Install a sanding belt and drape the power cord over your shoulder to keep it out of the way. With the sanding direction parallel to the wood grain, turn on the tool and slowly lower it onto the surface *(above)*. Some woodworkers prefer to set the tool flat on the workpiece before starting it. In either case, move the machine along the grain with long, overlapping strokes until the surface is smooth. To avoid gouging the surface, keep the sander flat and always moving; do not let the machine pause in one spot.

SHOP TIP

Making repeat cuts with the table saw

To cut several boards to the same length on the table saw, screw a board to the miter gauge as an extension, ensuring that one end extends beyond the saw blade. Push the miter gauge to cut into the end of the extension. Turn off the saw and mark the length of cut on the extension. Align a wood block with the mark and clamp it in place as a stop block. To line up each cut, butt the end of the workpiece against the block and make the cut.

CABINETMAKING JOINERY

This section introduces some standard joinery techniques common to the building of virtually any style of cabinet or bookcase. If you are using solid lumber for your project, you will make up the wide panels for the carcase or the panel of a frame-and-panel assembly by gluing boards together edge-to-edge, as shown below. This technique enables you to save money—wide boards are prohibitively expensive—without sacrificing strength; a glued-up panel is just as strong as a single piece of lumber. If you are working with plywood panels, hardwood banding will hide unsightly edges (page 25).

Of the dozens of joinery options, the through dovetail joint remains the benchmark of craftsmanship. The joint can be cut on a variety of power tools, but the hand-cutting technique shown starting on page 26 will give you the distinctive look associated with fine furniture. A plate joint, shown beginning on page 29, is a much quicker option. Although it lacks the dovetail's esthetic appeal, the plate joint is virtually as strong and is an excellent choice if you are working with plywood panels, which cannot be joined with dovetails. Whichever joint you choose, your carcase will need a back. Installation details are provided on page 31.

Many types of cabinets, including the armoire shown on page 60, are built around frame-and-panel assemblies rather than carcases. Two joinery options for building such a cabinet are presented: the mortise-and-tenon (page 33) and the cope-and-stick joint (page 35). The panels for a frame-and-panel cabinet can be raised on either the table saw (page 36) or router (page 38).

The plate, or biscuit, joint offers a strong and simple method of connecting carcase corners with a minimum of set-up time. The slots are cut with a special tool known as a plate joiner. Once glue is added to the slots, oval biscuits of compressed beech are inserted. When the joint is glued and assembled, the biscuits swell, creating a durable connection.

GLUING UP A PANEL

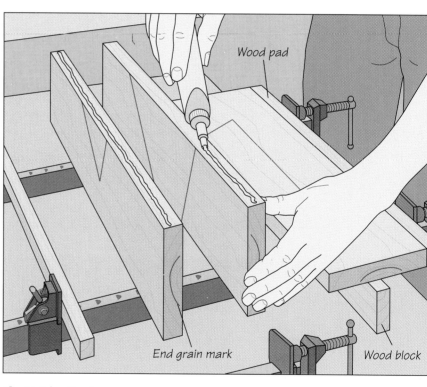

Wood pad

End grain mark

Wood block

1 Applying the glue
Set two bar clamps on a work surface and lay the boards on top. Add as many clamps as you need to support the pieces at 24- to 36-inch intervals. Prop the clamps on notched wood blocks to keep them from falling over. Mark the end grain orientation of each board with a pencil, then arrange the pieces to enhance their appearance, as shown in the photo on page 13. To minimize warping, make sure the end grain of adjacent boards runs in opposite directions. Once you have a satisfactory arrangement, align the pieces edge-to-edge and mark a triangle on the stock to help you assemble the boards at glue up. Next, cut two protective wood pads at least as long as the boards. Leaving the first board face down, stand the other pieces on edge with the alignment marks facing away from you. Apply a thin glue bead to each board (above), then use a small, stiff-bristled brush to spread the adhesive evenly.

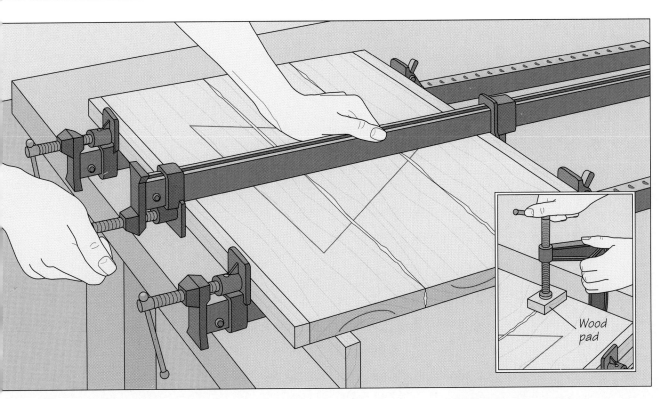

Wood pad

2 Tightening the clamps

Set the boards face down, making sure the sides of the triangle align. Tighten the clamps under the boards just enough to press them together. Install a third clamp across the top of the stock, centering it between the others. Gradually tighten all the clamps *(above)* until there are no gaps between the boards and a thin bead of glue squeezes out of the joints. Use a C clamp to level adjacent boards that do not lie perfectly flush with each other. Protecting the boards with a wood pad, center the clamp on the joint near the ends and tighten it until the boards are level *(inset)*, then remove the clamp and pad. Use a putty knife to remove as much of the squeezed-out glue as possible before it dries. Once the adhesive has cured, remove the clamps and use a paint scraper to remove any glue that remains.

SHOP TIP

Adding edge molding to plywood

Conceal the visible edges of plywood panels with solid-wood molding. Use a tongue-and-groove joint to join the pieces. Cut a groove into the edge one-third as thick as the panel. Then saw a matching tongue on the edge of the hardwood board that will be used as the edge molding. (It is best to make the tongue in a wide board, and then rip the molding from the piece). Secure the panel upright in a vise and spread some glue in the groove and on the tongue. Secure the molding in place with three-way clamps.

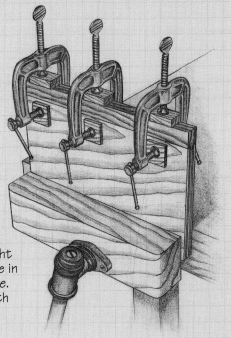

HAND-CUT DOVETAILS

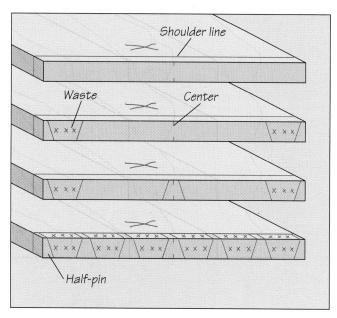

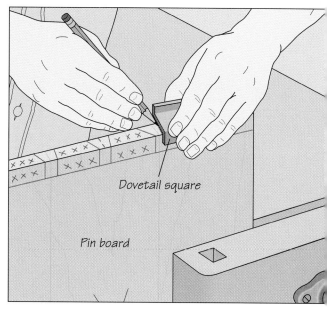

1 Outlining the pins

Mark the outside face of each board with a big X, then set a cutting gauge to the thickness of the stock and scribe a line around the ends of the four panels to mark the shoulder of the pins and tails. The panels that will form the top and bottom of the carcase will be the pin boards. Secure each one in turn in a vise and use a dovetail square to outline the pins on the ends of the board in the sequence shown above. (You can also use a sliding bevel to mark the pins; set an angle of 1:6 for softwood or 1:8 for hardwood.) There are no firm guidelines for sizing and spacing the pins of a dovetail joint. In general, the pins should be no wider than the tails; evenly spaced pins at least one-third the size of the waste sections around them will make for an attractive, strong joint. Begin with half-pins at each edge, making certain that the narrow sides of the pins are on the outside face of the panel. Outline the waste sections beside the half-pins and mark the center of the panel end. Outline a pin at the center mark, then mark the remaining pins *(above, right)*, indicating all the waste sections with Xs. Use a combination square to extend the marks down to the shoulder line on both faces as you go.

2 Cutting the pins

Secure the first pin board in a vise with its outside face toward you. Use a dovetail saw to cut along the edges of the pins, working from one side of the panel to the other *(right)*. Some woodworkers find it easier to cut all the left-hand edges first, and then move on to the right-hand edges. For each cut, align the saw blade with the waste side of the cutting line and use smooth, even strokes, taking care to keep the blade perpendicular to the panel end as you cut to the shoulder lines. Repeat the procedure at the opposite end of the board and at both ends of the other pin board.

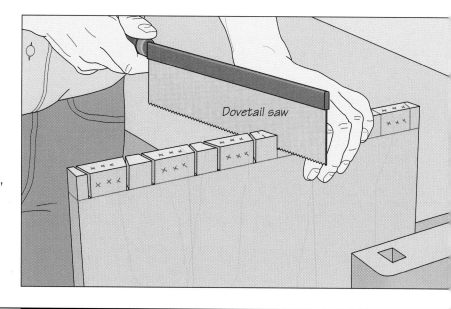

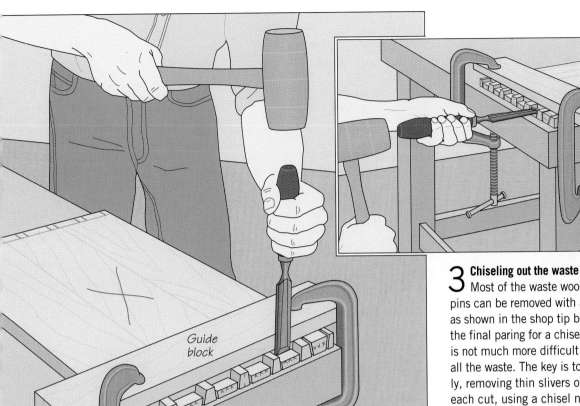

3 Chiseling out the waste

Most of the waste wood between the pins can be removed with a coping saw, as shown in the shop tip below, leaving the final paring for a chisel. However, it is not much more difficult to chisel out all the waste. The key is to work patiently, removing thin slivers of wood with each cut, using a chisel no wider than the narrow side of the waste section. Set the pin board outside-face up on a work surface and clamp a guide block on top with the edge aligned with the shoulder line. Holding the chisel bevel-out against the guide block and perpendicular to the face of the workpiece, strike the handle with a wooden mallet to score a ⅛-inch-deep cut *(above, left)*. Then cut from the end of the board to shave off a ⅛-inch layer of waste *(above, right)*. Continue removing the waste until you are about halfway through the stock. Once you have removed all the waste from one side of the board, turn it over, reposition the edge of the guide block directly over the shoulder line, and remove the waste from the other side.

Guide block

SHOP TIP

Cutting away waste with a coping saw

A coping saw works as well as a chisel for clearing away the bulk of the waste wood between the pins. With the panel secured upright in a vise, stand facing the outside face of the panel and slide the saw blade into the kerf beside each pin. Rotate the frame without striking the end of the board and cut out as much waste as you can while keeping the blade about ⅟₁₆ inch above the shoulder line. Cut until you reach the kerf on the edge of the adjacent pin. Use a chisel to pare away any remaining waste.

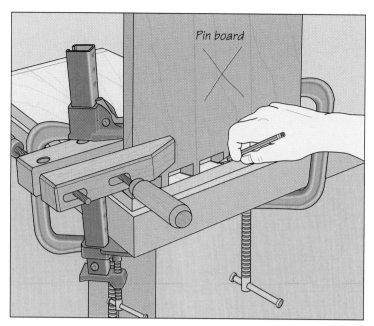

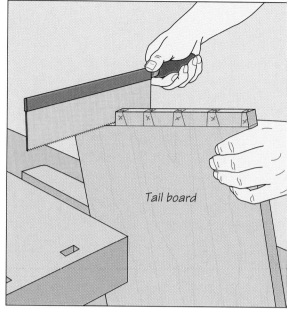

4 Outlining and cutting the tails

Mark shoulder lines on the tail boards as you did on the pin boards. Set one of the tail boards outside-face down on a work surface and clamp a guide block along the exposed shoulder line. Then, using a handscrew and clamps, fix one pin board on end against the guide block with its outside face away from the tail board. Make sure the edges are aligned, then outline the tails *(above, left)*. Repeat the procedure on the opposite end of the board and on the other tail panel, then remove the clamps and use a combination square to extend the lines onto the ends of the boards. Mark all the waste sections with Xs. Use a dovetail saw to cut the tails the same way you cut the pins *(step 2)*. For some woodworkers, angling the board *(above, right)* rather than the saw makes for easier cutting. In either case, saw smoothly and evenly along the edge of each tail, stopping at the shoulder line. Once all the saw cuts have been made in both tail panels, remove the waste with a chisel or a coping saw.

5 Gluing up the carcase

Dry-assemble the carcase before glue up to ensure the joints fit properly. Press each corner together by hand as far as it will go, then tap the pieces into final position with the mallet, protecting the wood with a scrap board. If a joint is too tight, mark the spot where it binds, then disassemble the carcase and pare excess wood at the mark. Once you are satisfied with the fit, take care of the other requirements of the carcase, such as installing a back panel *(page 31)* or preparing the sides for shelving or drawers. For glue up, make four wood pads as long as the width of the panels and cut small triangular notches in the pads so they only contact the tails. Spread a thin, even layer of glue on all the contacting surfaces, then assemble the carcase and install two bar clamps across the pin boards. Tighten the clamps a little at a time until a small amount of glue squeezes out of the joints *(right)*.

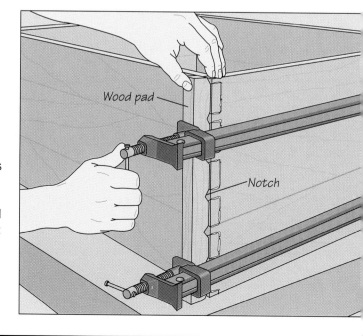

SSEMBLING A CARCASE WITH PLATE JOINTS

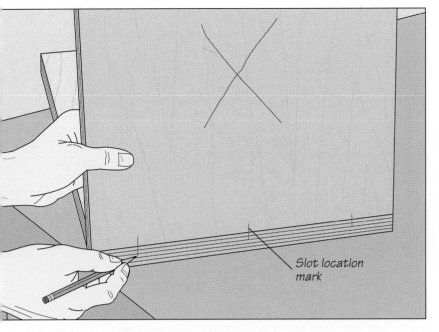

Slot location mark

1 Marking the slot locations
Identify the outside face of each panel with an X, then mark location lines for the slots on each of the four corners. To start, place one side panel outside-face down on a work surface and hold the top panel at a 90° angle to it. Use a pencil to mark lines on the adjoining panels about 2 inches in from each corner; make a third mark midway along the edge *(left)*. Wider panels will require additional biscuits; in general, there should be one biscuit every 4 to 6 inches. Repeat the procedure to mark slot locations on the other three corners of the carcase. Add reference letters to help you identify the corners.

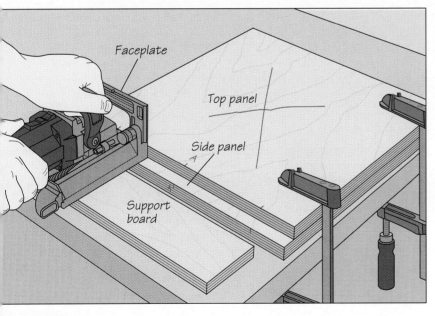

Faceplate

Top panel

Side panel

Support board

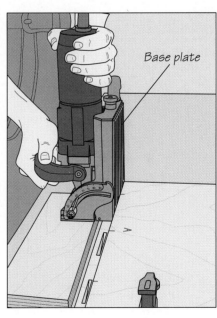

Base plate

2 Cutting the slots
The setup shown above will allow you to cut all the slots for ne carcase corner without moving the panels. Leaving a side anel outside-face down, set the top piece outside-face up on p of it. Offset the top panel by the stock thickness, making ure the mating slot location marks on the two panels are perctly aligned. Clamp the pieces in place and set a support oard the same thickness as the stock in front of the panels. ollow the manufacturer's instructions for setting the depth of

cut on the plate joiner. Rest the tool on the support board, butt its faceplate against the end of the top panel, and align the guideline on the faceplate with a slot location mark on the stock. Then cut a slot at each mark *(above, left)*. To cut the mating slots in the side panel, butt the joiner's base plate against the top panel and then align the center guideline on the plate with a slot location mark *(above, right)*.

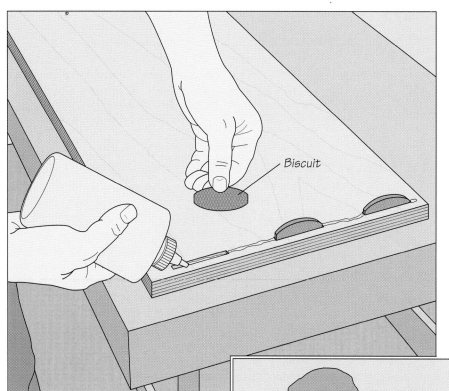

Biscuit

3 Inserting the biscuits
Once all the slots have been cut, dry-fit the panels and cut a back panel if that is part of your design *(page 31)*, or make ready for shelves or drawers. Then set one side panel outside-face down on the work surface and spread glue in the slots and along the panel surface, inserting biscuits as you go *(left)*. To prevent the wooden wafers from expanding before the panels are assembled, proceed to step 4 as quickly as possible.

4 Gluing up the carcase
Fit the top and bottom panels on the side panel and then apply adhesive in the slots and along the panel ends, inserting biscuits as you go. Add the other side panel *(right)*. Turning the carcase on end, use two bar clamps to press the top and bottom panels together and tighten the clamps exactly as you would when gluing up a carcase with dovetail joints *(page 28)*, this time using standard wood pads to protect the stock.

Top

ISTALLING A BACK PANEL

Support board

1 Routing a rabbet for the panel

Dry-assemble the panels and set the carcase on a work surface with its back facing up; hold the pieces together using a bar clamp with support boards. Install a ⅜-inch rabbeting bit with a ball-bearing pilot and adjust the depth of cut to make a rabbet that will be ¹⁄₁₆ inch deeper than the thickness of the back panel you will be installing. Starting at one corner of the carcase, rest the router's base plate on the support board with the bit just clear of the workpiece. Holding the router firmly in both hands, turn on the tool and guide the bit into the panel. Once the pilot bearing meets the stock, pull the router against the direction of bit rotation, keeping the base plate flat. When you reach the corner, turn off the tool, reposition the support board and cut rabbets along the edges of the remaining panels following the same procedure (left).

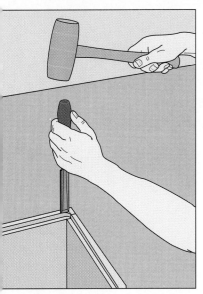

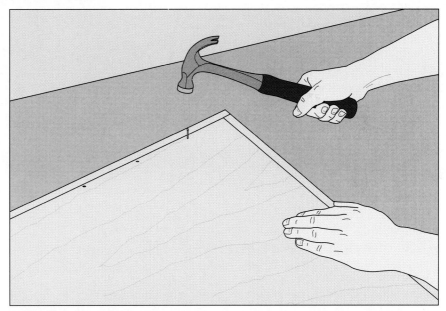

2 Squaring the corners

Use a pencil and a straightedge to mark square corners at the rounded ends of the rabbets. Using a ½-inch or der wood chisel, strike the tool with wooden mallet (above), cutting to the epth of the rabbet. Be sure the chisel evel faces the inside of the carcase.

3 Installing the panel

Installing the panel during glue up of the carcase will help keep the assembly square. Cut a piece of plywood to fit snugly into the rabbets. Glue up the carcase and, at the same time, apply a thin bead of glue along the rabbets and on the contacting surfaces of the plywood. Spread the glue evenly, set the panel in position, and use finishing nails to secure it at 4- to 6-inch intervals (above). You can also glue up the carcase separately, let the adhesive dry, and then install the panel.

FRAME-AND-PANEL CONSTRUCTION

Frame-and-panel cabinets may vary widely in their details, but all share several features: The assemblies are comprised of frames made from stiles and rails, and panels that fit into grooves in the frame. A typical front and side section is shown below at right. To provide access to the inside of the cabinet, the front frequently has a frame but no panel. This one features a median rail with openings for a door and a drawer. The two missing assemblies would be similar to the side assembly shown; each has a frame and a panel. In this case, the sides would share stiles with the front and back assemblies, allowing the rails to fit into both the edges and faces of the stiles.

Bottoms are typically attached to the frame by ledger strips or let into grooves cut in the inside edges of the frame. Tops can be attached with wood buttons that fit in grooves in the frame, or with metal fasteners, ledger strips, or pocket holes.

The two most common joints used in frame-and-panel construction are the mortise-and-tenon shown in the illustration and the cope-and-stick. The mortise-and-tenon provides a relatively large gluing area, making it a very strong joint. Two variations are employed in the typical cabinet: Blind mortise-and-tenons join median rails and stiles, while the haunched version is used to fill the groove end, eliminating the need for stopped grooves. The cope-and-stick is not quite as strong, but offers an additional decorative touch. The router bit that cuts the grooves for the panel also carves a decorative molding on the inside edges of the frame. Step-by-step techniques for producing these joints are shown in this section: the mortise-and-tenons starting on page 33 and the

cope-and-stick on page 35. Whatever the joint, cabinetmakers generally build frames from stock that is at least ¾ inch thick and 2 inches wide. Larger stock can also be used to suit the dimensions of a particular project.

The panels that fit inside the frames can be made either of plywood or edge-glued boards *(page 24)*. To ensure that a panel will fit snugly in the grooves of the rails and stiles, but still have a little room to move as the wood expands and contracts, it is made substantially thin-

ner on the edges than in the middle. The shape of such a so-called raised panel is achieved by cutting away thickness at the edges.

There are several ways of making a raised panel, depending on the visual effect you desire. A common method, shown beginning on page 36, involves beveling the edges of the panel with a table saw or router.

The steps for gluing up individual frame-and-panel assemblies and cabinets are shown on page 39.

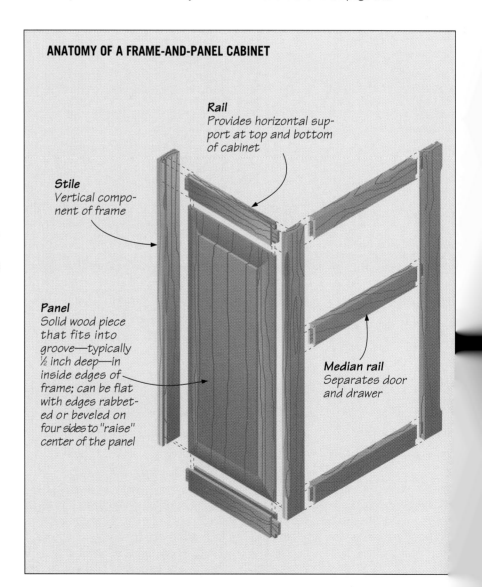

ANATOMY OF A FRAME-AND-PANEL CABINET

Rail
Provides horizontal support at top and bottom of cabinet

Stile
Vertical component of frame

Panel
Solid wood piece that fits into groove—typically ½ inch deep—in inside edges of frame; can be flat with edges rabbeted or beveled on four sides to "raise" center of the panel

Median rail
Separates door and drawer

MORTISE-AND-TENON JOINTS

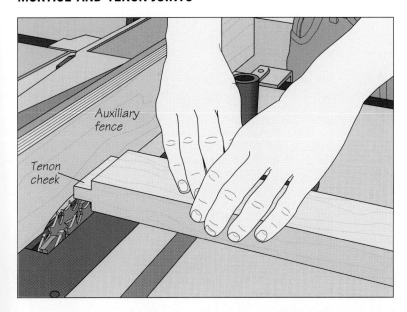

1 Cutting the tenon cheeks in the rails

For both blind and haunched tenons, start by installing a dado head on your table saw that is slightly wider than the length of the tenons—often ¾ inch. Then attach an auxiliary fence and raise the blades to cut a clearance notch in it. Set the width of cut equal to the tenon length and the cutting height to one-third the stock thickness. Feed the workpiece face-down, butting the end against the fence and the edge against the miter gauge. Turn the rail over and repeat the cut on the other side *(left)*. Test the tenon in a scrap piece of wood with a mortise the same width as those to be cut in the stiles *(page 34)*; adjust the height of the dado head and repeat the cuts, if necessary. Cut the remaining tenon cheeks before proceeding.

2 Cutting the tenon shoulders

The shoulders for both blind and haunched tenons can be cut on the table saw. For the blind tenons, leave the cutting width unchanged and set the height of the dado head to about ⅛ inch. With the rail flush against the fence and the miter gauge, feed the workpiece on edge into the blades. Turn the rail over and repeat on the other side of the tenon *(above)*. Cut the shoulders at the opposite end of the rail the same way. For the haunched tenons, use the same cutting height and cut one shoulder as for the blind tenons, then position the fence to leave a haunch equal in width to the depth of the panel groove on the other shoulder. With the stock on edge, use the fence and the miter gauge to feed it into the blades *(inset)*. Repeat to cut the haunch on the other end of the board.

3 Routing the mortises

Clamp all the stiles together face to face, ends aligned, and use one of the blind tenons cut in step 2 to outline the mortises on the stiles. To cut each mortise, secure one stile in a vise. Install a commercial edge guide on a plunge router, then screw a wood extension onto the guide. Fit the router with a straight bit the same width as the mortise and set the cutting depth. Center the bit over the mortise outline and butt the extension against the stile. Gripping the router firmly, turn it on and plunge the bit into the stock *(right)*. Move the tool from one end of the mortise to the other, making as many passes as necessary to complete the cut to the required depth. Repeat to rout the other mortises, then square the ends of the cavities with a chisel.

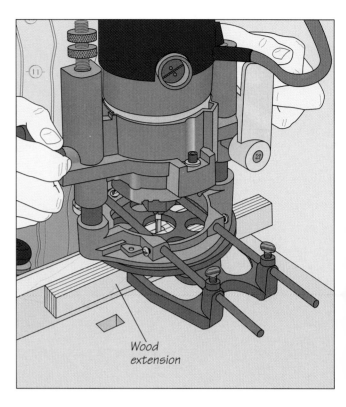

Wood extension

Push stick

Featherboard

Guard

4 Cutting the grooves

On the rails and stiles of each frame, mark the location of the grooves that will hold the panel. Leave the straight mortising bit in the router, mount the tool in a table, and adjust the cutting depth to about ½ inch. Center the edge of a stile on the bit and butt the fence against the stock. Clamp a featherboard to the table to hold the workpiece against the fence and feed the stock with both hands, making sure to press the stile flush against the fence *(left)*. Complete the pass with a push stick. To cut grooves in the stile faces, keep the fence in the same position, but reposition the featherboard as necessary. Next, you can cut and raise the panels *(page 36)*.

A COPE-AND-STICK CABINET

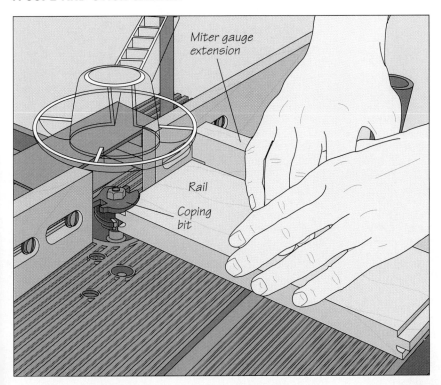

Miter gauge
extension

Rail

Coping
bit

1 Cutting the tongues in the rails

Begin constructing a cope-and-stick frame by cutting tongues in the ends of all the rails. After that, rout grooves for the panels along the inside edges of the frame pieces; the grooves in the stiles will accommodate the rail tongues at the same time. To cut the tongues, install a piloted coping bit—the rail cutter—in your router and mount the tool in a table. Set the cutting depth by butting the end of a rail against the bit and adjusting the router's depth setting so that the top of the uppermost cutter is slightly above the workpiece. Position the fence parallel to the miter gauge slot and in line with the edge of the bit pilot. Fit the miter gauge with an extension and lay the outside face of the stock flat on the table; keep the ends of the workpiece and extension butted against the fence throughout each cut *(left)*.

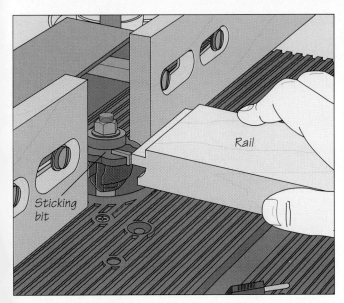

Rail

Sticking
bit

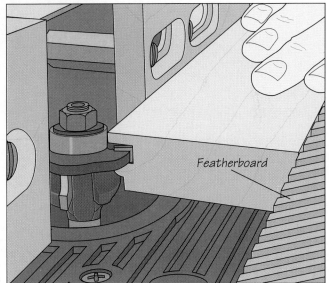

Featherboard

2 Cutting the grooves

Replace the coping bit with a piloted sticking bit—also known as a stile cutter. To set the cutting depth, butt the end of the completed rail against the bit, and adjust the bit until one of its groove-cutting teeth is level with the rail tongue *(above, left)*. Align the fence with the edge of the pilot bearing. Use two featherboards to secure the workpiece during the cut:

Clamp one to the router table opposite the bit and secure the other on the infeed side of the fence. (In this illustration, the second featherboard has been removed for clarity.) Make each cut with the stock outside-face down, pressing the workpiece against the fence *(above, right)*. Use a push stick to complete the pass. Repeat the groove cut on all the rails and stiles.

RAISING A PANEL WITH A TABLE SAW

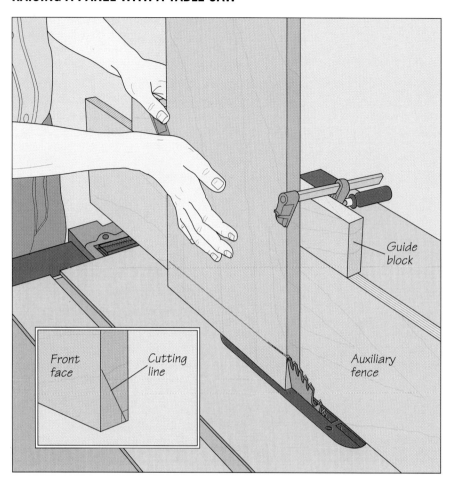

Front face   Cutting line

Guide block

Auxiliary fence

1 Cutting the end grain
Test-fit the rails and stiles and measure the opening between them. Add ½ inch to each dimension; ¼ inch of each panel side will fit into the grooves in the frame. Then cut the panel to size on the table saw. To determine the blade angle for raising the panel, draw a ¼-inch square at the bottom corner, then mark a line from the front face of the panel through the inside corner of the square to a point on the bottom edge ⅛ inch from the back face *(inset)*. Hold the panel against an auxiliary wood fence and adjust the blade angle until it aligns with the marked line. Adjust the height of the cutting edge until the outside tip of one tooth extends beyond the face of the panel, then clamp a guide block to the workpiece to ride along the top of the fence. Feed the panel into the blade, keeping it flush against the fence while pushing it forward with the guide block *(left)*. Test-fit the cut end in a groove. If less than ¼ inch of the panel enters the groove, move the fence a little closer to the blade and make another pass. Repeat the cut at the other end of the panel.

2 Cutting with the grain
Set the panel on edge and feed it into the blade, then turn the panel over to cut the remaining edge *(right)*. No guide block is needed for these cuts, but take care to keep the back flush against the fence. Cutting into the end grain of the panel first—beveling the top and bottom before the sides—helps reduce tearout.

A JIG FOR CUTTING RAISED PANELS

The jig shown at right will enable you to raise a panel on the table saw without having to tilt the saw blade. Refer to the illustration for suggested dimensions.

Screw the lip along the bottom edge of the angled fence, making certain to position the screws where they will not be struck by the blade when the jig is used. Lean the angled fence against the auxiliary fence at the same angle as the cutting line marked on the panel *(page 36)*. (Use a sliding bevel to transfer the angle.) Cut triangular supports to fit between the two fences and fasten them in place with screws.

To use the jig, set it on the saw table with the seam between the lip and the angled fence over the blade; check to be sure the screws are well

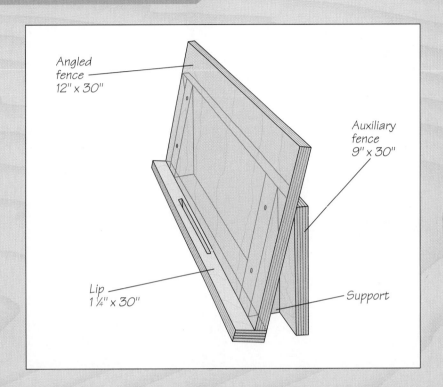

Angled fence
12" x 30"

Auxiliary fence
9" x 30"

Lip
1 ¼" x 30"

Support

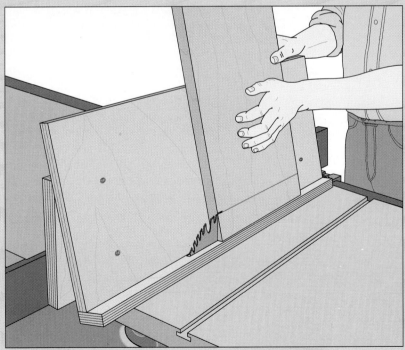

clear of the table opening. Position the rip fence against the auxiliary fence, then screw the two together. Turn on the saw and crank up the blade slowly into the jig to cut a kerf through the lip. Turn off the saw, seat the panel in the jig and adjust the blade height until the outside tip of one tooth extends beyond the front face of the panel. Make a test cut on a scrap board the same thickness as the panel, then test-fit the cut end in a groove. Reposition the blade or fence, if necessary. Then, place the panel in the jig and make the cuts, beveling the end grain first *(left)*.

MAKING A RAISED PANEL WITH A ROUTER

1 Setting up the router

Install a panel-raising bit in your router and mount the tool in a table. To ensure that the cutting depth is uniform, position the fence parallel to the miter gauge slot and in line with the bit pilot. With the router turned off, adjust the fence by placing a scrap board along the fence and across the bit. The bit pilot should turn as the board touches it *(right)*. Start with a ⅛-inch-deep cut so that you will reach your final depth in two or more passes.

Bit pilot

Guard

2 Raising the panel

Lower the guard over the bit and turn on the router. To minimize tearout, cut the end grain of the panel first. Work carefully; a panel-raising bit is one of the more dangerous router bits because of the large amount of stock that it removes with each pass. Keep the panel flat on the table outside-face down and flush against the fence as you feed it across the bit *(left)*. Repeat the cut at the other end and along both sides. Turn off the router and test-fit one end in a frame groove. If the panel lies less than ¼ inch deep in the groove, increase the cutting depth slightly and make another pass all around. Continue in this manner until the panel fits properly.

ASSEMBLING A FRAME-AND-PANEL CABINET

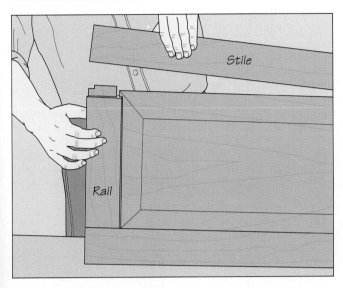

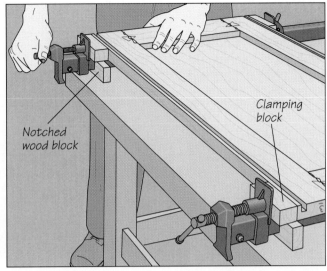

1 Gluing up a single assembly

Test-assemble the frame-and-panel *(above, left)*. If a joint is too tight, disassemble the pieces and use a chisel to pare away some wood. Once you are satisfied with the fit, sand any surfaces that will be difficult to reach when the frame has been glued up, and spread glue on all the contacting surfaces of the joints. Do not apply any adhesive in the panel grooves; the panel must be free to move within the frame. Reassemble the frame and set it face down on two bar clamps, aligning the bars with the rails. To keep the clamps from falling over, prop them up in notched blocks. Using clamping blocks to protect the stock, tighten each clamp in turn until a thin bead of glue squeezes out of the joints *(above, right)*. Check that the corners are at 90° as you go. Once the adhesive has dried, remove any dried glue remaining on the wood with a paint scraper, and sand the outside surfaces.

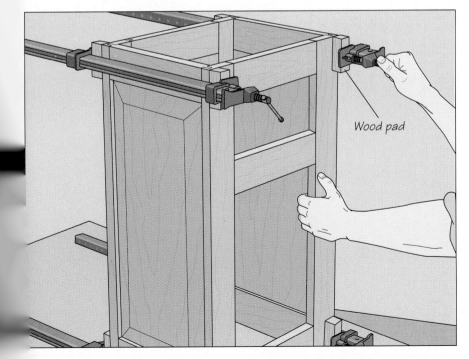

2 Gluing up the cabinet

Test-fit the cabinet, adjust any ill-fitting joints, and sand the inside surfaces of all the pieces. Apply glue to the joints—except the grooves that hold the panels—and assemble the cabinet. Then, with the cabinet upright, install four bar clamps running from front to back over the rails, using wood pads to protect the stock. Tighten the clamps evenly *(left)* until a thin bead of glue squeezes out of the joints. Check that the cabinet is square by measuring the distance between diagonal corners; the two measurements should be the same. If not, install an extra bar clamp across the longer of the two diagonals, setting the clamp jaws on those already in place. Tighten the clamp until the diagonals are equal. Once the glue has cured, remove the clamps and scrape away any dried adhesive.

BOOKCASE

A length of molding is shaped on a router table. Fixed to the base or the top of the carcase, molding provides a classic touch to a bookcase.

Whether it is a simple plywood structure or a custom-made wall unit crafted from fine hardwood, a bookcase serves two functions at once: It is an efficient storage system, accommodating books and other items that accumulate in most homes, and a fine piece of furniture in its own right, as handsome as the freestanding unit at left.

The basic bookcase illustrated on page 42 can be adapted to store just about anything, from bound volumes to china, crystal, toys, records, compact discs, and videocassettes. With the addition of some specialized hardware *(page 44)*, a simple bookcase can be transformed into a home entertainment center to house a television and VCR, stereo components and computer gear. This utilitarian versatility makes the bookcase one of the woodshop's most popular projects.

Although the appearance of a bookcase may vary from one unit to another, the principles of its design remain constant. Every bookcase must strike a balance between its size and the size and weight of the items it is intended to hold. Shelves, for example, must be long enough to do their job, but not so long that they will sag in use. Shelves can be fixed in place or adjustable. Each has its own advantages. Adjustable shelving *(page 45)* permits a more flexible organization of a bookcase's interior space, but fixed shelves *(page 50)* lend a bookcase structural rigidity.

You have considerable choice of building materials, joinery methods, and ornamentation when building a bookcase. The chapter that follows details the construction of a basic unit. You may wish to add a face frame to strengthen the piece and soften its lines *(page 54)*. Molded bases and feet *(page 56)* can allow a bookcase to harmonize with other pieces of furniture that will surround it. See page 59 for a simple method of stringing a series of bookcases together into a wall unit.

By putting your imagination, skill, and patience to work, you will be able to reap the rewards of building a fine piece of useful furniture.

Because books come in many shapes and sizes, bookcases with adjustable shelves retain their flexibility long after they are built. With all but one of its shelves movable, the bookcase at left can accommodate the changing demands of a growing collection.

ANATOMY OF A BOOKCASE

Despite refinements such as crown and base molding, a face frame and turned feet, the bookcase at right is basically a carcase with shelves. The procedure for building a carcase can be found beginning on page 24. Most of the other details of the bookcase, from the shelves to the feet, are discussed in this chapter. The crown molding is similar to the type installed on the armoire on page 66.

Design a bookcase to suit the items it will store. Standard bookshelves, for example, are at least 8 inches deep and 9 inches apart; allow an additional 3 or 4 inches of depth and height for oversize books. Record albums need 13 inches in both depth and height. Televisions, video recorders, and stereo equipment may require up to 24 inches of depth.

After you have settled on dimensions, decide which type of shelving best suits your needs. The bookcase on this page features three adjustable, or floating, shelves and one fixed shelf. Although the fixed shelf cannot be moved once installed, it helps to strengthen the piece and is less likely to sag than adjustable shelves. The load the shelves will have to bear should be considered when choosing materials *(page 43)*. The thicker the lumber, the stronger the shelf. While 1-by-10 pine or fir is economical, ¾ hardwood will support greater loads.

Also remember that a shelf weakens as it increases in length. Shelves that are too long are not likely to break, but they will almost always sag. If you are planning a bookcase wider than 36 inches, consider installing cleats under the middle of the shelves at the back or a vertical partition between them.

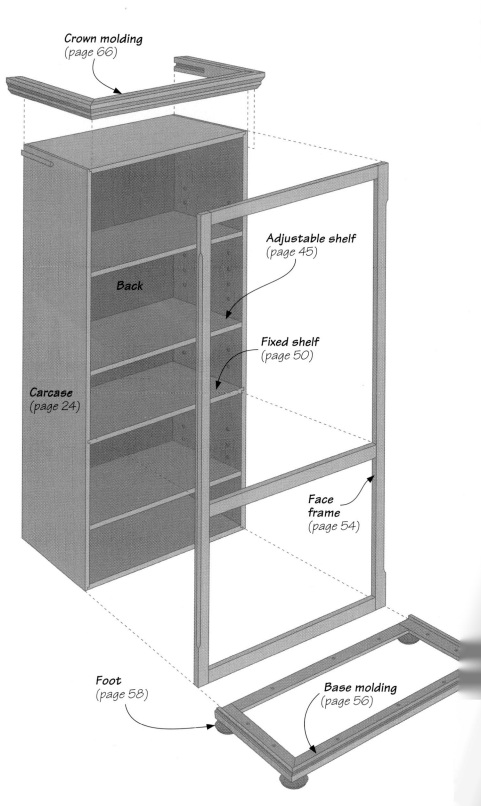

Crown molding
(page 66)

Adjustable shelf
(page 45)

Back

Fixed shelf
(page 50)

Carcase
(page 24)

Face frame
(page 54)

Foot
(page 58)

Base molding
(page 56)

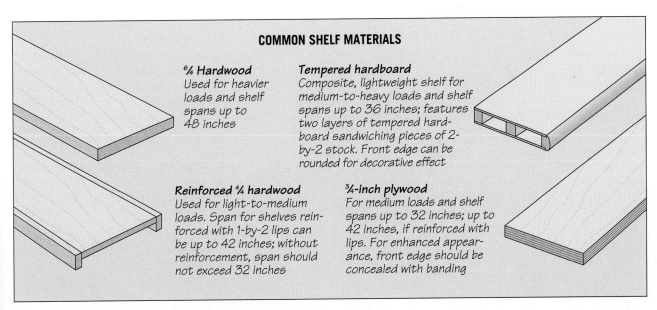

COMMON SHELF MATERIALS

⁶/₄ Hardwood
Used for heavier loads and shelf spans up to 48 inches

Tempered hardboard
Composite, lightweight shelf for medium-to-heavy loads and shelf spans up to 36 inches; features two layers of tempered hardboard sandwiching pieces of 2-by-2 stock. Front edge can be rounded for decorative effect

Reinforced ¼ hardwood
Used for light-to-medium loads. Span for shelves reinforced with 1-by-2 lips can be up to 42 inches; without reinforcement, span should not exceed 32 inches

¾-inch plywood
For medium loads and shelf spans up to 32 inches; up to 42 inches, if reinforced with lips. For enhanced appearance, front edge should be concealed with banding

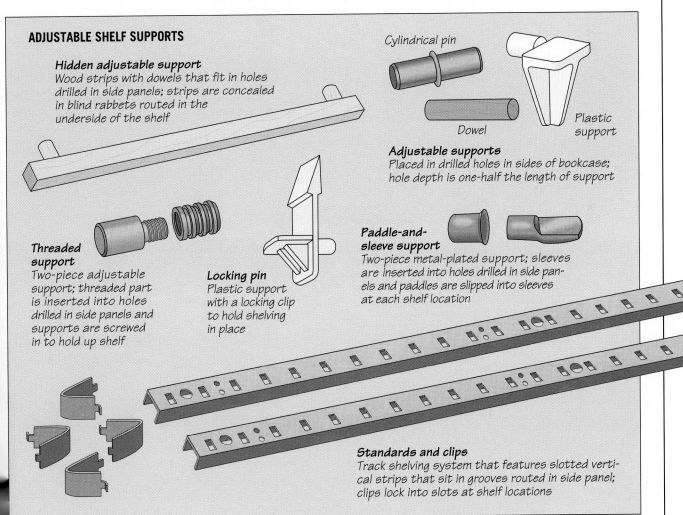

ADJUSTABLE SHELF SUPPORTS

Hidden adjustable support
Wood strips with dowels that fit in holes drilled in side panels; strips are concealed in blind rabbets routed in the underside of the shelf

Cylindrical pin

Dowel

Plastic support

Adjustable supports
Placed in drilled holes in sides of bookcase; hole depth is one-half the length of support

Threaded support
Two-piece adjustable support; threaded part is inserted into holes drilled in side panels and supports are screwed in to hold up shelf

Locking pin
Plastic support with a locking clip to hold shelving in place

Paddle-and-sleeve support
Two-piece metal-plated support; sleeves are inserted into holes drilled in side panels and paddles are slipped into sleeves at each shelf location

Standards and clips
Track shelving system that features slotted vertical strips that sit in grooves routed in side panel; clips lock into slots at shelf locations

BOOKCASE ACCESSORIES

Books are not the only items commonly stored in a bookcase. With the commercial accessories shown below, you can easily organize record albums, compact discs, audio tapes, and videocassettes. If you intend your bookcase to house a stereo system, television or

VCR, wire clips and cord-hole plugs can tame the tangle of wires and connectors that accompany them.

Specialty items like runners let you slide shelves in and out of the carcase, providing easy access to the contents, while swivel attachments can be installed

on a sliding shelf or the bookcase top for a television set.

You can even illuminate the inside of your bookcase with a cabinet light or hide and protect the contents behind tinted glass or acrylic doors held closed by magnetic latches.

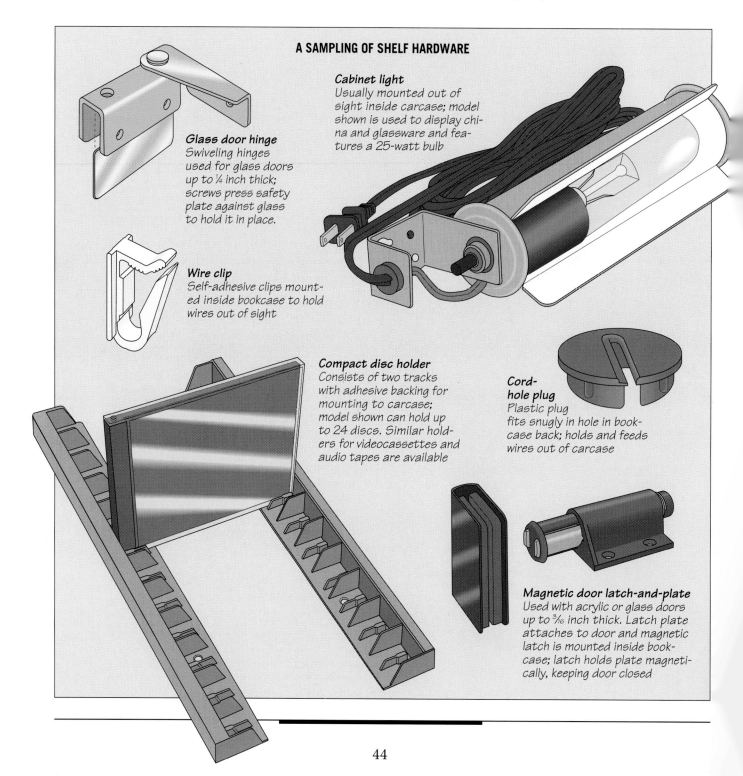

A SAMPLING OF SHELF HARDWARE

Glass door hinge
Swiveling hinges used for glass doors up to ¼ inch thick; screws press safety plate against glass to hold it in place.

Cabinet light
Usually mounted out of sight inside carcase; model shown is used to display china and glassware and features a 25-watt bulb

Wire clip
Self-adhesive clips mounted inside bookcase to hold wires out of sight

Compact disc holder
Consists of two tracks with adhesive backing for mounting to carcase; model shown can hold up to 24 discs. Similar holders for videocassettes and audio tapes are available

Cord-hole plug
Plastic plug fits snugly in hole in bookcase back; holds and feeds wires out of carcase

Magnetic door latch-and-plate
Used with acrylic or glass doors up to ⅜ inch thick. Latch plate attaches to door and magnetic latch is mounted inside bookcase; latch holds plate magnetically, keeping door closed

ADJUSTABLE SHELVING

Although adjustable shelves do not contribute to the strength of a bookcase, they do give it greater flexibility, allowing you to adapt to changing needs and organize space most efficiently. It is unwise to make a bookcase without providing at least one fixed shelf for structural rigidity.

Adjustable shelves are commonly held in place with wood, plastic, or metal shelf supports *(page 43)* that fit in holes drilled in the carcase sides. The trick is to make certain that the rows of holes are perfectly aligned. Use a commercial shelf-drilling jig *(below)* or a shop-made jig *(page 46)* to bore the holes. Other options include adjustable shelf standards, which are mounted in grooves in the side panels, or shop-made corner strips *(page 48)*. These are dadoed and attached to the interior corners of the bookcase to hold up the shelving.

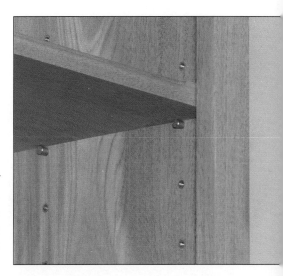

Made of solid brass, these two-piece shelf supports add an elegant touch to a bookcase. The supports can be screwed into any of the threaded sleeves along the side panels, permitting the shelves to be mounted at any height in the bookcase.

THREADED SHELF SUPPORTS

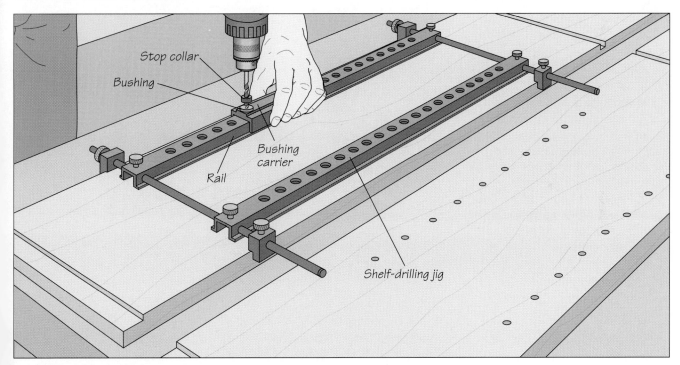

Stop collar

Bushing

Bushing carrier

Rail

Shelf-drilling jig

1 Drilling holes for the sleeves

This mounting system requires two parallel rows of holes to be drilled in the side panels of the bookcase. The commercial jig shown above allows you to bore holes at 1-inch intervals and ensures that corresponding holes will be perfectly aligned. Set the side panels inside-face-up on a work surface and clamp the jig to the edges of one panel; the holes can be any distance from the panel edges, but about 2 inches in would be best for the panels shown. Fit your electric drill with a bit the same diameter as the sleeves and install a stop collar to mark the drilling depth equal to the sleeve length. Starting at either end of one of the jig's rails, place the appropriate bushing in the first hole of the bushing carrier. (The bushing keeps the bit perfectly square to the workpiece.) Holding the drill and carrier, bore the hole. Bore a series of evenly spaced holes along both rails. Remove the jig and repeat for the other side panel, carefully positioning the jig so that the holes will be aligned with those in the first panel.

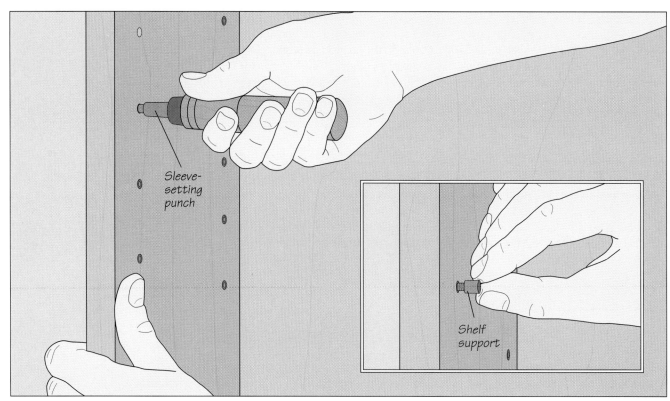

Sleeve-
setting
punch

Shelf
support

2 **Mounting the sleeves and supports**
To install threaded sleeves without damaging them, use a sleeve-setting punch. Place a sleeve on the end of the punch and push it firmly into one of the holes in a side panel *(above)*. Insert a sleeve into each hole you drilled. Once you have installed all the sleeves, screw shelf supports into the sleeves at each shelf location *(inset)*.

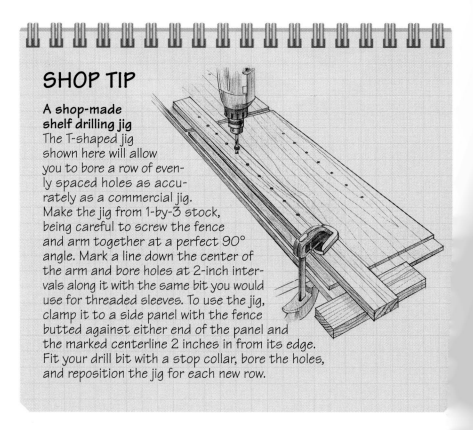

SHOP TIP

**A shop-made
shelf drilling jig**
The T-shaped jig
shown here will allow
you to bore a row of evenly spaced holes as accu-
rately as a commercial jig.
Make the jig from 1-by-3 stock,
being careful to screw the fence
and arm together at a perfect 90°
angle. Mark a line down the center of
the arm and bore holes at 2-inch intervals along it with the same bit you would
use for threaded sleeves. To use the jig,
clamp it to a side panel with the fence
butted against either end of the panel and
the marked centerline 2 inches in from its edge.
Fit your drill bit with a stop collar, bore the holes,
and reposition the jig for each new row.

HIDDEN SHELF SUPPORTS

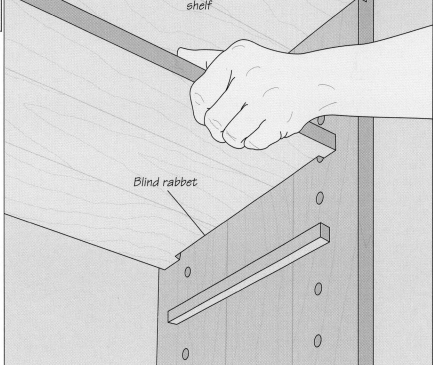

1 Making and installing the shelf supports

Use a jig to bore holes for the shelf supports *(page 45)*. Make two supports per shelf. Each one is a thin wood strip about 1 inch longer than the gap between the rows of holes; make the strip wide enough to hold a dowel at each end. (⅜-inch dowels are large enough for average loads.) To help you position the dowels on the supports, insert a dowel center into each of two parallel holes and press the strip against the points. Use the indentations from the centers as starting points for drilling the holes. Make the holes in the shelf supports the same depth as the holes in the side panels. Glue dowels into the shelf supports and, once the adhesive has dried, install them on the side panels at the height that you want the shelf to rest *(left)*.

Shelf support

Fixed shelf

Blind rabbet

2 Preparing and installing the shelves

To conceal the shelf supports, cut blind rabbets in each shelf. Mark out the rabbets by positioning the shelf on the supports and outlining their locations on the underside of the shelf. Cut the rabbets using a router fitted with a rabbeting bit and square the ends with a chisel and a wooden mallet. The rabbets should be as deep as the thickness of the shelf supports. Once all the rabbets have been cut, test-fit the shelf in the bookcase *(right)*. Use a chisel to adjust the rabbets, if necessary, to ensure a perfect fit that completely hides the supports.

47

STANDARDS AND CLIPS

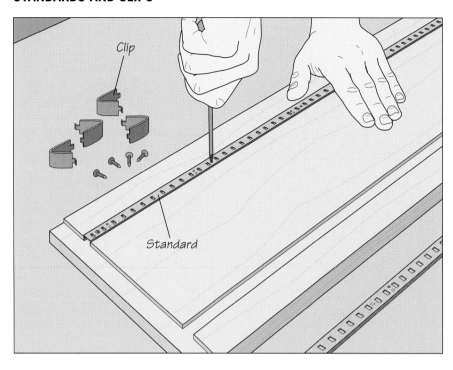

Installing the standards

Metal standards and clips are among the simplest accessories to install for mounting adjustable shelves in a bookcase. Two slotted standards, or tracks, are fastened to the inside faces of the side panels and shelf-support clips are inserted in the slots at the desired height. Rather than notching the shelves to accommodate the standards, recess the tracks in grooves cut in the side panels. Install a dado blade on your table saw and cut two parallel grooves in each panel. The grooves should be as wide and as deep as the standards; for the width of panel shown, position the grooves about 2 inches in from each edge. With the panels inside-face-up on a work surface, set the standards in the grooves and fix them in place, driving screws through the predrilled holes in the tracks *(left)*. Attach clips to the standards at each shelf location.

CORNER STRIPS

1 Making the corner strips

Dadoed corner strips installed in each inside corner allow bookcase shelves to be adjusted. You can make four strips from a single 4-inch-wide board that is long enough to extend from top to bottom of the interior. Install a dado head on your table saw and set the width equal to the thickness of the shelf supports you plan to use. Determine the desired spacing of the notches and cut two dadoes that distance apart in a miter gauge extension board. Line up the left-hand dado with the blade and screw the extension to your gauge. One dado should be offset to the right; cut a 2-inch piece of shelf support stock and press it into that dado, where it will serve as an indexing key. Butt one end of the workpiece against the key and cut your first dado. Cut the second and subsequent dadoes by moving the piece to the right and fitting the last dado over the key *(right)*. When the dadoes are all cut, rip the board into four 1-inch corner strips.

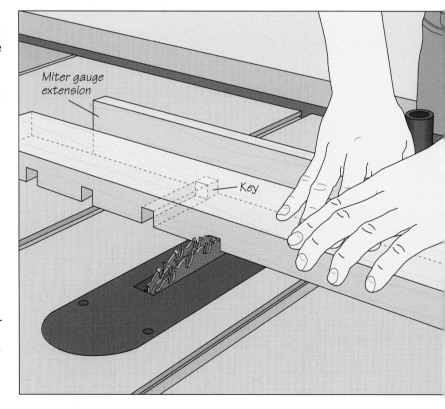

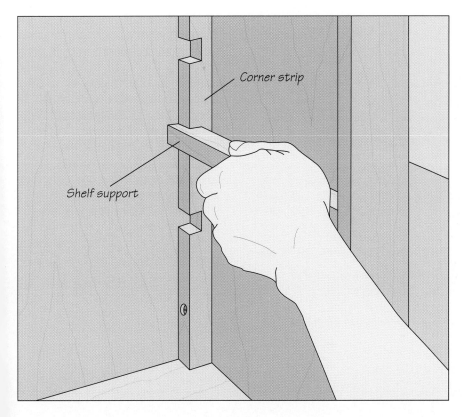

Corner strip

Shelf support

2 Installing the corner strips and shelf supports

Position each strip in a corner of the bookcase, making sure that the dadoes face the interior, and screw the strips to the sides at top and bottom. Place an extra fastener in the middle on a tall bookcase. For the shelf supports, measure the distance between the front and back of the bookcase and cut the supports to fit. Make sure that the supports are wide enough to hold the shelves properly; test-fit them to ensure that they fit snugly in the dadoes (left).

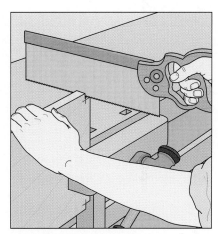

3 Preparing the shelves

All four corners of each shelf must be notched to fit around the corner strips. After measuring and marking each shelf, secure it in a vise and cut out the corners with a backsaw (above).

SHOP TIP

Jig for routing evenly spaced dadoes
Attach the jig shown here to the base plate of your router to cut the dadoes in the corner strips of a shelf support system. (This technique can also be used to rout dadoes for fixed shelves.) Make the base from ½-inch plywood and the spacer from solid wood. Cut a bit clearance hole through the base and screw it to the router. Make the width of the spacer equal to the diameter of the straight bit you will use to cut the dadoes. Screw the spacer to the bottom of the jig base so the distance between it and the bit equals the spacing you want between the dadoes. Cut the first dado with the spacer riding along the end of the workpiece. Make subsequent cuts with the spacer in the just-cut dado.

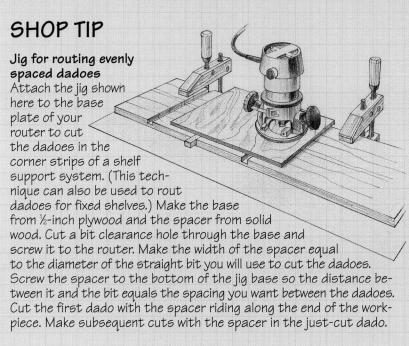

FIXED SHELVES

Fixed shelves bolster the structur[al] integrity of a bookcase, but sin[ce] they cannot be moved once they a[re] installed, you need to give caref[ul] thought to their location. You ca[n] mount fixed shelves quite simply [by] screwing them to cleats that are fasten[ed] to the back and side panels. Your boo[k]case will be stronger and more attra[c]tive, however, if the shelves are attache[d] to the side panels using one of the joi[n]ery methods shown below.

If you do not intend to add a fa[ce] frame to your bookcase, remember th[at] some of these joints will conceal the c[ut] made in the side panel for the shelf.

Cutting through dadoes in the side panels is one of the quickest ways to join a fixed shelf to a bookcase. In the photo above, the side panels are clamped together with their ends flush, allowing two perfectly aligned dadoes to be cut at the same time. A straightedge jig guides the router through the cut.

JOINERY OPTIONS FOR FIXED SHELVING

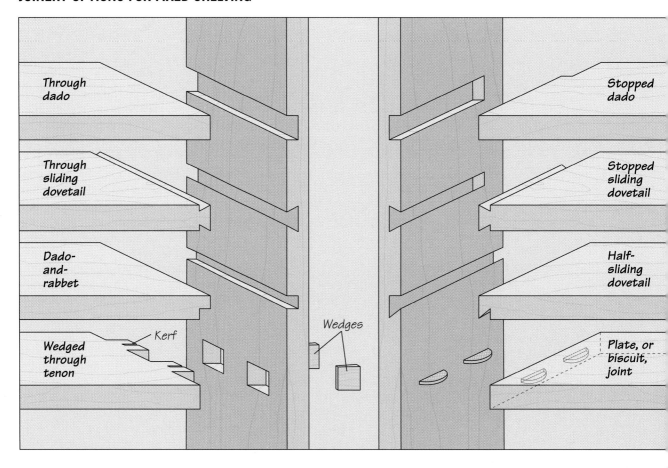

Through dado

Through sliding dovetail

Dado-and-rabbet

Wedged through tenon

Kerf

Wedges

Stopped dado

Stopped sliding dovetail

Half-sliding dovetail

Plate, or biscuit, joint

MAKING A HALF-SLIDING DOVETAIL

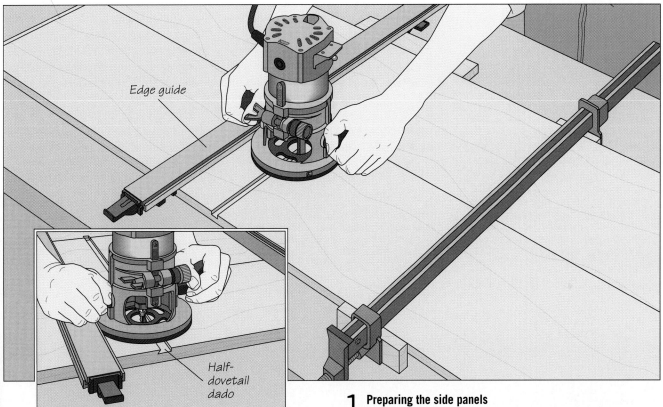

Edge guide

Half-dovetail dado

1 Preparing the side panels

The half-dovetail dadoes in the side panels are routed in two steps: first with a straight bit, and then with a dovetail bit. Install a straight bit of the desired diameter in your router. Clamp the side panels edge-to-edge and inside-face-up to a work surface; make sure their ends are aligned. Clamp a board against the stock at the end of the cutting line to prevent tearout. Also clamp an edge guide across the panels, offset to properly locate the edge of the router base plate and the bit. Starting at one edge of the panels, feed the router across the stock, pressing the base plate against the edge guide throughout the cut *(above)*. Complete the dado by making the second cut with a dovetail bit *(inset)*, shifting the edge guide away from the first cut by one-half the dovetail bit diameter.

2 Preparing the shelf

To create mating half-dovetail tongues on the ends of the shelves, leave the dovetail bit in the router and mount the tool in a table. Position the fence for a shallow cut. Feed the shelf on end into the bit, keeping it flush against the fence with one hand while pushing it forward with the other hand *(left)*. Test-fit the cut end in a half-dovetail dado. Adjust the fit, if necessary, by moving the fence $\frac{1}{16}$ inch away from the bit and making another pass. Repeat the cut at the other end of the shelf.

EDGE TREATMENTS FOR SHELVES

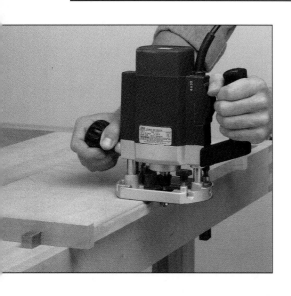

Edge treatments are strips of solid wood, veneer, or commercial banding applied to the visible edges of plywood shelves; they conceal the panels' plies, creating the illusion that the shelving is made of solid wood. Commercial edge banding is available by the roll in a wide variety of wood types, colors, and widths. To install, simply cut off the length you need, set it in place, and heat it with a household iron to melt the adhesive that bonds it to the ed of the shelf.

Although a little more painstaki to apply, shop-made wood strips off several advantages over store-boug banding. They are often less costly, ar you can finish your shelf edges wi any available wood species, cut whatever thickness you desire. A va ety of solid wood edge treatments shown below.

If your shelves are made of solid wood, you can rout a decorative design in their edges. For plywood shelves you will need to attach wood strips or veneer to cover the plies.

A SELECTION OF EDGE TREATMENTS

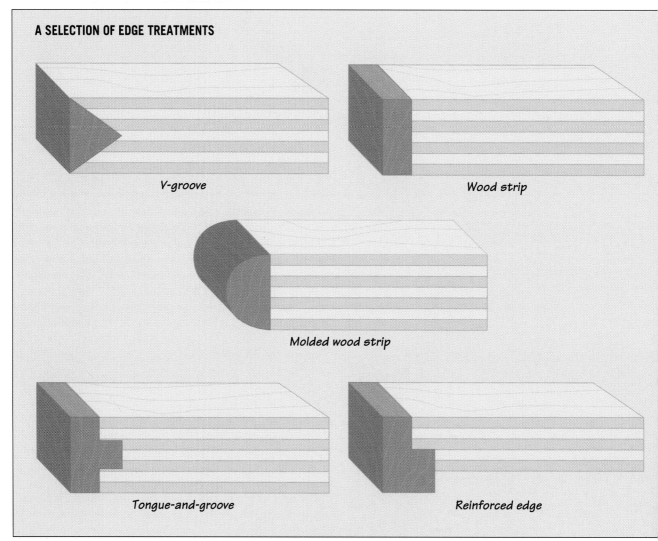

V-groove

Wood strip

Molded wood strip

Tongue-and-groove

Reinforced edge

EINFORCING A SHELF

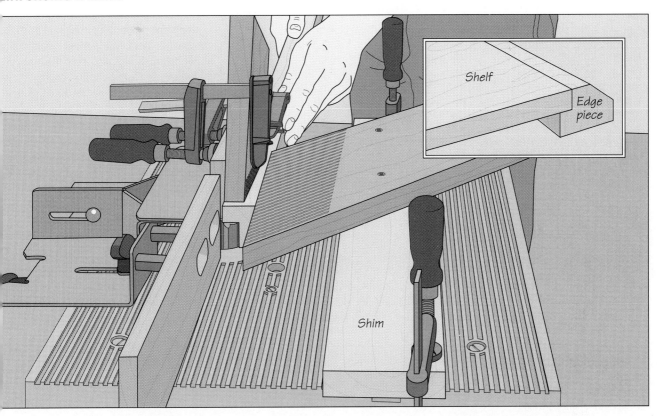

Shelf

Edge piece

Shim

Rabbeting the edge piece

A piece of hardwood can be glued to the edge of a shelf to strengthen it. To rout the rabbet in the edge piece, install a ¾-inch straight bit in your router and mount the tool in a table. Set the fence for a width of cut equal to the thickness of the shelf. To secure the workpiece through-out the cut, screw a featherboard to a shim and clamp the assembly to the table. The shim will raise the feather-board to apply pressure to the middle of the workpiece. Also install featherboards to the fence on both sides of the bit. (For the sake of clarity, the featherboard on the outfeed side of the fence has been removed in the illustration.) Do not attempt to rout the rabbet in one pass; instead, make a series of passes, increas-ing the depth of cut each time *(above)*. Repeat until the shelf fits flush in the rabbet *(inset)*. You can round or shape the edge piece to your liking.

SHOP TIP

Springboard clamp for edge gluing
For thick edge treat-ments, you might need three or four clamps to hold the piece in place while the glue dries. A single clamp will do the job just as well if you use a spring-board. To make the device, cut a gentle curve—¼-inch-deep at its center—along one edge of a 2-inch-wide board the same length and thickness as the panel. Center the panel on top of the bar clamp and set the concave edge of the springboard against the edge material. Using a wood pad to protect the other edge of the panel, tighten the clamp until the springboard flattens against the edge.

FACE FRAMES

Because they completely cover the edges of side panels, face frames are ideally suited for plywood bookcase construction. Made from a contrasting wood, they can also provide a decorative detail. Cutting and assembling a face frame demands precision; the joints must be tight and the frame square if it is to fit properly and provide strength. Use the assembled carcase as a reference to measure the rails and stiles. Face frames are either glued in place or attached with biscuit joints as shown below.

A face frame strengthens a carcase while hiding panel edges. It also provides jambs for door hinges.

INSTALLING A FACE FRAME

1 Cutting slots in the carcase and face frame

Measure your carcase and cut the two rails and stiles of the face frame to length; also cut median rails to cover any fixed shelves. The frame should rest flush with the outside of the carcase. Join the rails and stiles with dowels, biscuits, or mortise-and-tenon joints, then glue up the face frame assembly, ensuring that it is square. Once the adhesive is dry, sand it and place it on top of the bookcase. Mark the locations of the biscuit joints on both the carcase and the face frame—typically every 4 to 6 inches. Set the plate joiner for the biscuit you are using and cut the slots in the carcase *(right)*, aligning the guideline on the face plate with each pencil mark. Then cut mating slots in the frame.

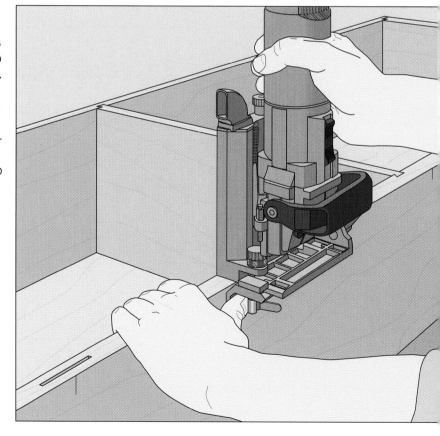

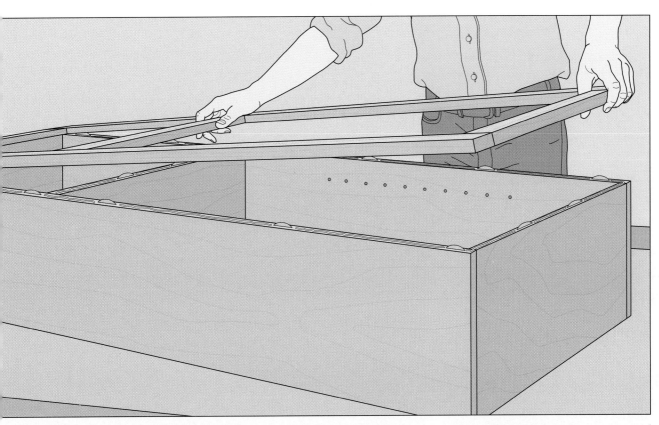

2 Installing the face frame

Apply glue to the slots in the carcase and face frame and along the mating surfaces. Insert the biscuits in the carcase slots, then set the face frame in place *(above)*. Work quickly since the glue will cause the biscuits to expand almost immediately.

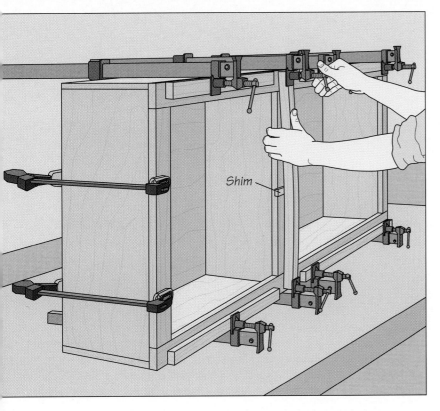

Shim

3 Clamping the assembly

Clamp the face frame to the carcase about every 12 inches. To apply pressure to the center of the median rail, use a piece of stock clamped to the carcase at either end with a shim in the middle *(left)*.

BASES AND FEET

Base molding is often added to a bookcase to "anchor" the piece and complement any crown molding installed the top. There are two basic ways to build a base. The first is to make a rabbeted mitered frame of molded pieces from stock standing on edge (see below); the frame wraps around the base of the bookcase like a skirt and hides the joinery at the bottom of the carcase. The second method involves building a mitered frame of horizontal molded stock; this provides a flat surface for attaching turned feet (page 58). Both methods allow for wood expansion and can also be adapted to fit modular bookcases or bookcases joined together.

Base molding and feet add a finishing touch to a bookcase. The molding can be routed to match the crown molding or the surrounding trim in the room.

INSTALLING A RABBETED BASE MOLDING

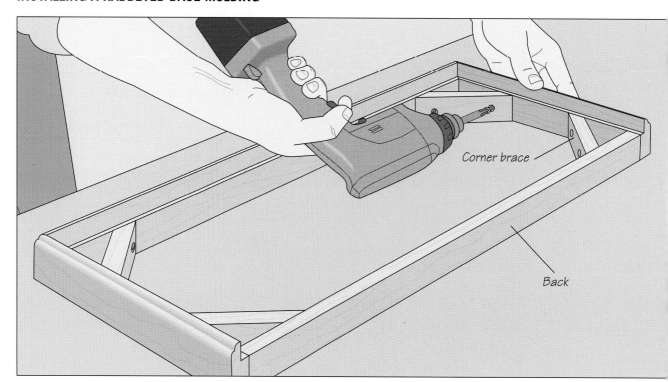

Corner brace

Back

1 Assembling the frame
The frame shown above is made from three pieces of molded stock, a back, and four corner braces. A rabbet is cut along the inside edge of the molded pieces, forming a lip that the bookcase will sit on. To make the base molding, first prepare three pieces of solid stock and rout a decorative molding in the edge of each. Then install a straight bit and cut a rabbet in the opposite face of each piece. Cut the molding to length with miters at both front corners, then cut a piece of stock for the back and join it to the sides with biscuits. Glue the front to the sides and screw corner braces in place to secure the joint (above).

2 Installing the base molding

Once you have finished assembling the frame, attach the unit to the bottom of the bookcase. To reinforce the joint, screw two angle brackets midway along the inside frame of the base molding. Spread glue on the rabbet on the front piece of the frame and on the first inch of the side pieces. (This will cause any wood movement to take place toward the back of the carcase, preventing the miter joints at the front from breaking.) Then set the frame in place on the bookcase, and screw the brackets to the bottom of the carcase.

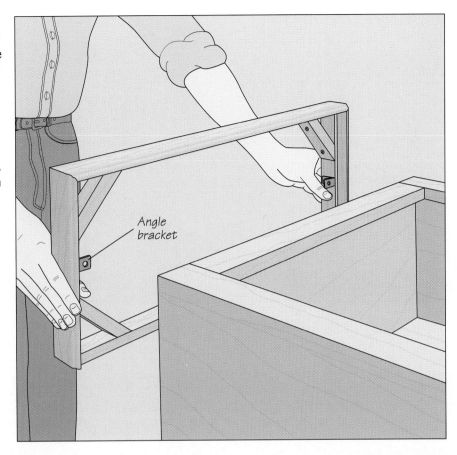

Angle bracket

BOTTOM BRACES, BASE MOLDINGS, AND FEET

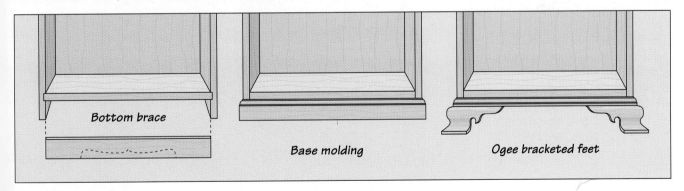

Bottom brace

Base molding

Ogee bracketed feet

Installing a bottom brace

If your bookshelf features no base molding and a fixed shelf is located near the bottom of the piece in place of a carcase bottom, you can install a bottom brace to hide the space below the shelf *(above, left)*. Simply cut the brace to size and glue or nail it in place from the ends and the top of the bottom shelf. You can also cut a decorative pattern in the brace *(dotted lines)*. A base molding *(above, center)* glued or screwed to the front and sides from inside the carcase is another option. You might also choose to attach ogee bracketed feet *(above, right)*. (See page 97 for more information on their construction and installation.)

INSTALLING A BASE WITH FEET

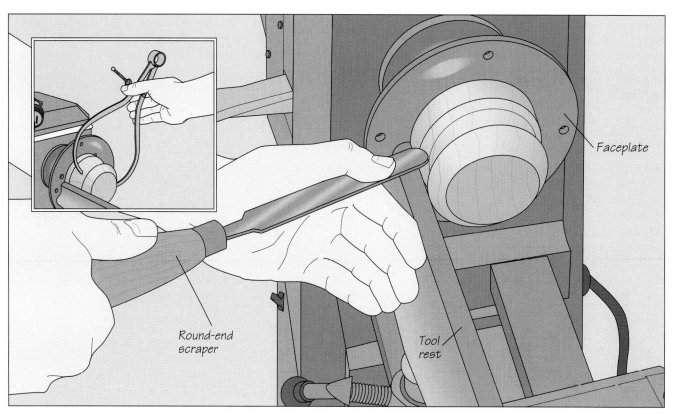

Round-end
scraper

Faceplate

Tool
rest

1 Turning the feet

Cut blanks for the feet from the appropriate size stock. To turn each blank, determine its center, mount the block on a faceplate, and attach the faceplate to the lathe. Position the tool rest in line with the center of the blank and as close to the stock as possible without touching it, then use a round-end scraper to shape the foot *(above)*. Always work on the "down" side of the spinning block to prevent kickback. Periodically check the profile of the foot with a pair of outside calipers *(inset)*. Once you are satisfied with its profile, sand the foot on the lathe with progressively finer sandpaper.

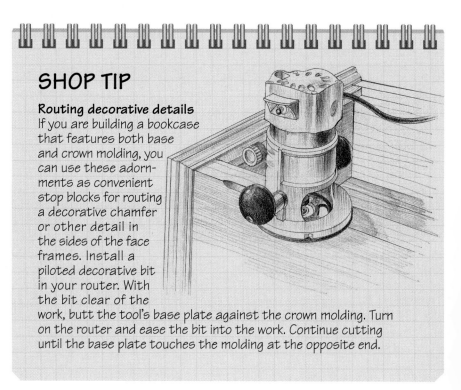

SHOP TIP

Routing decorative details
If you are building a bookcase that features both base and crown molding, you can use these adornments as convenient stop blocks for routing a decorative chamfer or other detail in the sides of the face frames. Install a piloted decorative bit in your router. With the bit clear of the work, butt the tool's base plate against the crown molding. Turn on the router and ease the bit into the work. Continue cutting until the base plate touches the molding at the opposite end.

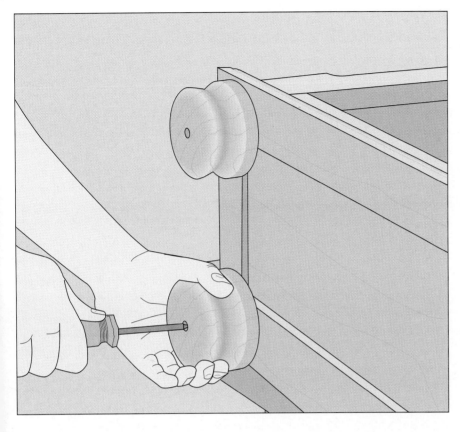

2 Installing the feet

Once you have turned all the feet, screw them to the bottom of the base molding. Unlike the vertical base molding shown on page 56, the base illustrated at left is horizontal, with a wide rabbet routed in the face of each piece that accepts the bottom of the bookcase; a molding is cut on the frame's outer edge *(page 96)*. After assembling the base, drill a countersunk hole three-quarters of the way through the center of each foot, then bore a pilot hole the rest of the way through the wood. Screw the feet to the base *(left)*.

ATTACHING BOOKCASES TOGETHER

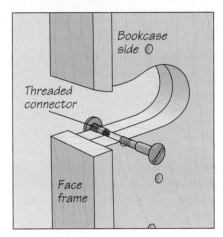

Using threaded connectors

If you are building more than one bookcase or a modular wall unit, consider attaching adjacent bookcases together for stability. A quick and efficient way to do the job is to use threaded connectors to join adjacent sides *(above)*. With the two bookcases side by side and properly aligned with each other, bore a hole through the two side panels. Install a threaded connector; for stability, use four to six connectors along the length of the side panels. If your bookcases have face frames, you can install intermediate stiles to hide the gap between the two bookcases.

SHOP TIP

Anchoring bookcases to the wall
Once stacked with books, magazines, and other items, bookcases can be dangerously top-heavy. Large, freestanding bookcases are best anchored to the wall, preferably to a stud. If your bookcase is tall enough, an angle bracket on top will be invisible. Or you can locate the angle bracket underneath the highest fixed shelf and screw it through the back panel and into the wall.

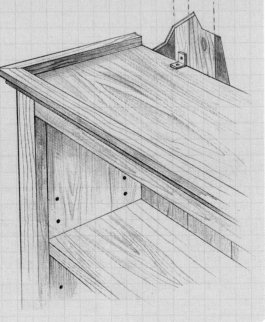

ARMOIRE

The armoire came into favor during the late 15th and early 16th Centuries to meet the growing need for storage space by Renaissance Europe's wealthy and acquisitive city dwellers. The armoire provided upright storage of fine goods; before, belongings were usually packed in large chests.

From the beginning, the armoire was as prized for its decorative attributes as for its practicality. The piece is essentially a freestanding closet featuring one or two doors, providing space to hang clothes, and occasionally drawers and shelving to furnish additional storage. The design reached a pinnacle in the late 17th Century, when Parisian cabinetmaker André-Charles Boulle produced several for the court of Louis XIV. Though his pieces were undeniably Baroque in their elaborate ornamentation, they still serve as loose models for the armoires of today.

In America, the term armoire is often interchanged with its English equivalent, wardrobe. By whatever name, the piece has proven to be popular in North America since the late 18th Century, and now it serves as everything from a food cupboard and a clothes closet to an entertainment center.

This glass curio, or display, cabinet was constructed in much the same way as the armoire on the facing page, except that the wooden shelves and the side and door panels were replaced with glass.

Whatever its use, the modern armoire is usually built in the traditional, or period, style. Like its ancestors, today's armoire begins with an upright, rectangular cabinet, typically 74 to 80 inches tall and 36 to 48 inches wide. For use as a wardrobe, the piece should be deep enough to house a clothes hanger—about 22 inches.

The basic cabinet shown on page 60 was put together with frame-and-panel joinery *(page 32)* to achieve a combination of attractiveness and strength. Dovetails *(page 26)* and plate joints *(page 29)* are equally sturdy alternatives.

This chapter shows how to add the adornments of an armoire to a basic cabinet: pilasters *(page 64)*, cornice and base moldings *(page 66)*, and frame-and-panel doors *(page 72)*. The elements of the armoire are highlighted in the anatomy on page 62.

Despite its elaborate appearance, the armoire is a reasonable project for a woodworker of average skills. Build the various pieces carefully and the result will be an attractive, versatile piece of furniture.

The armoire at left displays a muted Baroque design typical of many modern American wardrobes.

ANATOMY OF AN ARMOIRE

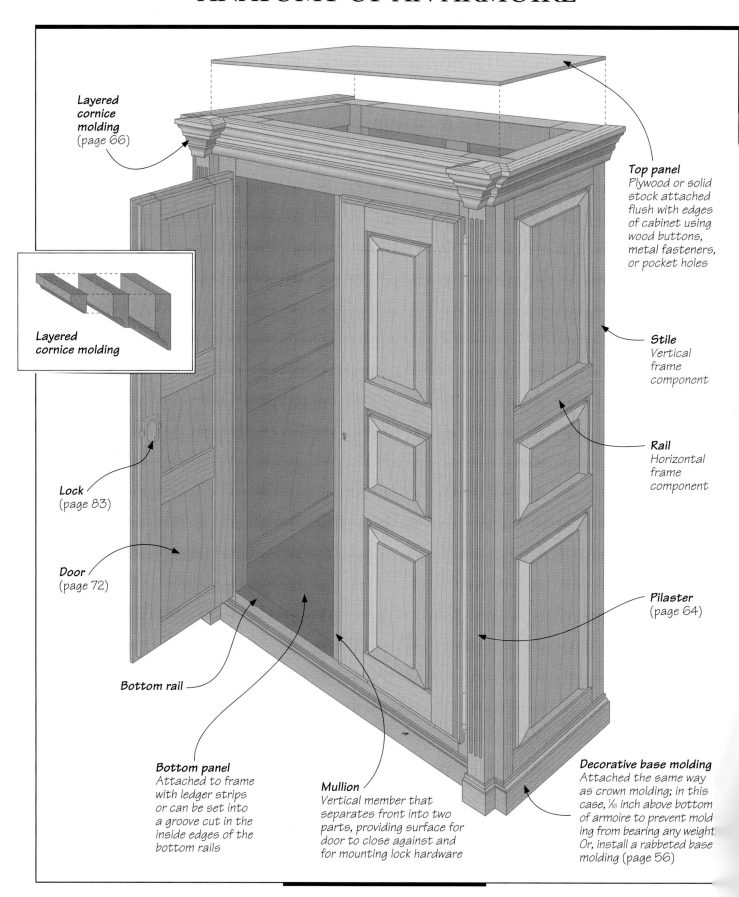

Layered cornice molding (page 66)

Layered cornice molding

Top panel
Plywood or solid stock attached flush with edges of cabinet using wood buttons, metal fasteners, or pocket holes

Stile
Vertical frame component

Rail
Horizontal frame component

Lock (page 83)

Door (page 72)

Pilaster (page 64)

Bottom rail

Bottom panel
Attached to frame with ledger strips or can be set into a groove cut in the inside edges of the bottom rails

Mullion
Vertical member that separates front into two parts, providing surface for door to close against and for mounting lock hardware

Decorative base molding
Attached the same way as crown molding; in this case, 1/16 inch above bottom of armoire to prevent molding from bearing any weight. Or, install a rabbeted base molding (page 56)

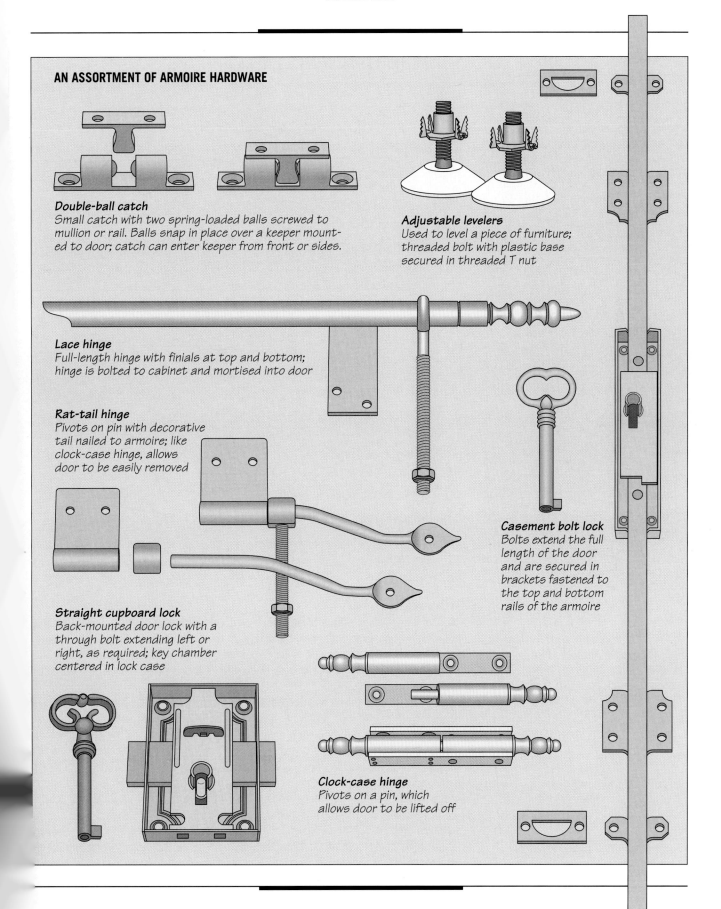

AN ASSORTMENT OF ARMOIRE HARDWARE

Double-ball catch
Small catch with two spring-loaded balls screwed to mullion or rail. Balls snap in place over a keeper mounted to door; catch can enter keeper from front or sides.

Adjustable levelers
Used to level a piece of furniture; threaded bolt with plastic base secured in threaded T nut

Lace hinge
Full-length hinge with finials at top and bottom; hinge is bolted to cabinet and mortised into door

Rat-tail hinge
Pivots on pin with decorative tail nailed to armoire; like clock-case hinge, allows door to be easily removed

Casement bolt lock
Bolts extend the full length of the door and are secured in brackets fastened to the top and bottom rails of the armoire

Straight cupboard lock
Back-mounted door lock with a through bolt extending left or right, as required; key chamber centered in lock case

Clock-case hinge
Pivots on a pin, which allows door to be lifted off

Pilasters are narrow boards fastened to the front stiles of an armoire and fluted with two or three blind grooves for decoration.

MAKING AND INSTALLING PILASTERS

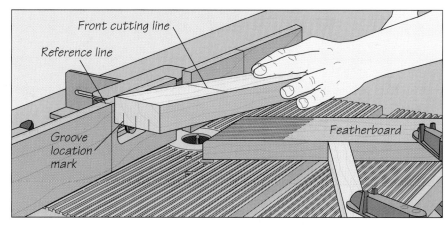

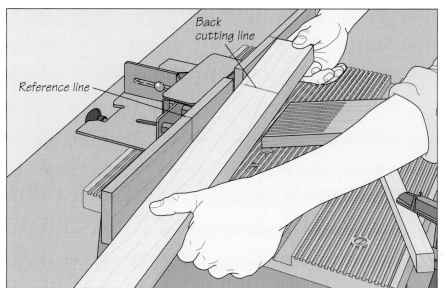

1 Cutting the grooves

Cut the pilaster pieces to size, taking into account the width of the stiles and allowing enough space between the door and the pilaster for the hinges you plan to use. Then, install a core box bit in your router and mount the tool in a table. Adjust the cutting height for a semicircular cove. Mark the location of the grooves on the end of the board and add marks on the face indicating where the cut should start and end. Align the front cutting line with the bit, then use the leading end of the piece to mark a reference line on the outfeed fence. Repeat the procedure with the back cutting line and make a similar reference line on the infeed fence. Adjust the fence for the first groove, then install a featherboard on the table to hold the pilaster firmly against the fence. Round over the top edge of the featherboard to prevent the stock from catching when it is pivoted down into the cut. To make the cuts, align the leading end of the pilaster with the reference line on the outfeed fence and lower the board face onto the bit *(above, top)*. Hold the workpiece flat on the table as you make your pass. When the back end of the piece aligns with the reference line on the infeed fence, pivot the stock off the table *(above, bottom)*. Repeat the cut on the other pilaster, then adjust the fence to cut the remaining grooves.

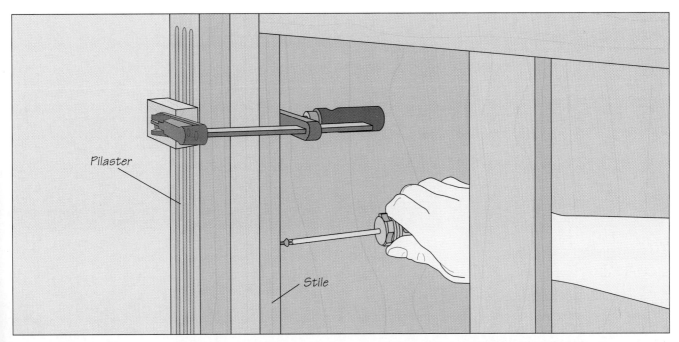

Pilaster

Stile

SHOP TIP

Shaping pilasters on the table saw

With the help of a simple shop-built jig, you can use the cove-cutting technique shown on page 69 to shape pilasters. For the jig, cut a wedge-shaped base piece at the appropriate angle for the cove you need and screw it to two fences: a low fence along one long side and a higher one on the adjacent side, then screw the jig to the saw's rip fence. To make the cuts, line up the middle of the leading end of a test board with the blade and adjust the rip fence until the angled guide butts against the pilaster. Turn on the saw and feed the board into the blade as shown; adjust the cutting height until you create the appropriate groove. Mark groove location lines and front and back cutting lines on the workpiece as you did in step 1 on page 64, then saw the grooves. Use extreme care in lowering and raising the work- piece at each end of the groove.

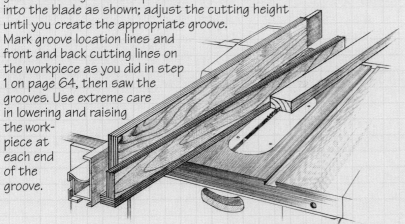

2 Installing the pilasters

Pilasters can be secured with glue alone, but for added strength, use some well-concealed screws. First, determine the location of the pilasters on the stile. They are typically centered between its edges. Next, spread a thin, even coat of glue on the back face of the pilaster, set it in place, and clamp it, using wood pads to protect the stock. Drill pilot holes into the pilaster from inside the cabinet and drive a screw into the top and bottom of the pilaster (above). Repeat the process to mount the second pilaster.

CORNICE MOLDINGS

Created by the three separate router bits shown below, the three layers of molding that make up the typical cornice at right appear as one single piece when they are installed on an armoire. Besides providing a visual framework for the armoire, the molding serves a second esthetic function, leading the eye into the center of the piece and keeping it focused there.

MAKING CORNICE MOLDING

LAYERED CORNICE MOLDING

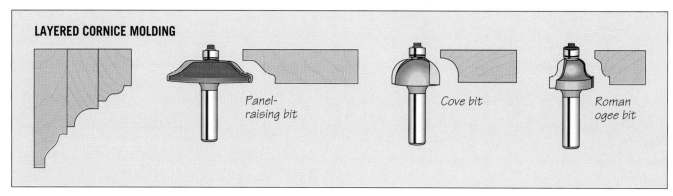

Panel-raising bit

Cove bit

Roman ogee bit

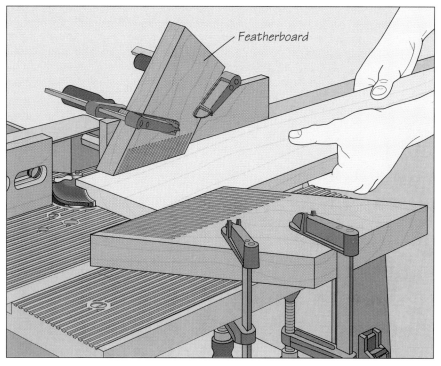

Featherboard

1 Routing the molding

Cut three boards longer and wider than you will need for the three layers of molding *(above)*. Install a panel-raising bit in your router and mount the tool in a table. Align the bit bearing with the fence and adjust the cutter height to leave a flat lip no more than ¼ inch thick on the edge of the stock above the molding. Mount two featherboards on the fence and one on the table to secure the stock throughout the cuts. (In this illustration, the featherboard on the outfeed fence has been removed for clarity.) Turn on the tool and feed the stock *(left)*. To complete the pass, move to the outfeed side of the table and pull the stock through the end of the cut. Make several passes, increasing the width of cut ⅛ inch of stock at a time. Form the second board with the cove bit and the third piece with the Roman ogee bit.

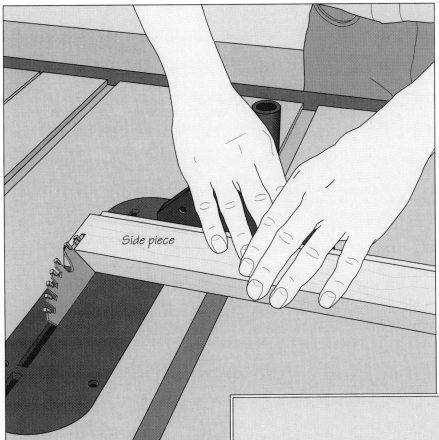

Side piece

2 Mitering the molding

When you have made the three molding strips, rip each to width (the first, innermost piece should be the widest and the third the narrowest). Then cut strips slightly longer than you will need for the front and sides of the workpiece. The ends of the molding strips are mitered at 45° to go around the corners and pilasters. The procedure for each layer is the same: Hold the side molding in position, its back end flush with the back of the cabinet. Mark the front corner of the cabinet on the strip. (For the second and third strips, mark the front corner of the previous layer of molding.) In addition, mark the direction required for the miter cut. Tilt the table saw blade to 45° and feed the stock using the miter gauge *(left)*. **(Caution: Blade guard removed for clarity.)** Repeat the cut on the second side piece. Then, mark and cut the ends of the front pieces.

3 Installing the first layer of molding

Each layer of molding is fastened to the armoire in two steps: The longer strips for the side and front are attached first, followed by the smaller pieces around the pilasters. Spread a thin layer of glue on the back face of the first side piece, then set it in place against the armoire with its top level with or slightly above the top of the cabinet. Use a cut-off brad as shown on page 123 to help position the molding while you clamp and screw it in place at either end of the strip. If you are using carcase rather than frame-and-panel construction to build the armoire, use a sliding dovetail to hold the side moldings in place *(page 127)*. Repeat the procedure to attach the other side molding, then mount the front piece *(right)*.

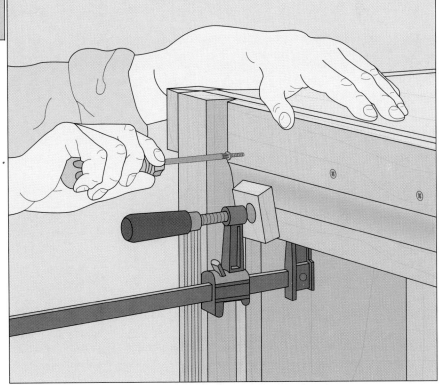

4 Applying the molding around the pilasters

Once the sides and main front piece of the first layer of molding are installed, the small pieces around the pilasters must be cut to size and mounted in place. Four small pieces need to be fitted around each pilaster; miter all the pieces at 45° at both ends. Hold the mitered end of a strip of the first molding flush against the mitered end of the main front piece, then mark the front corner of the pilaster on the edge of the molding. Make a 45° miter cut at this point. Then, hold the molding in place and repeat the procedure to mark and cut the next piece. Continue in this manner until the four pieces are cut to surround each pilaster. Dry-assemble the pieces to ensure an accurate fit, then spread glue on the pieces and fit them in place. Secure the front piece on the pilaster with a screw. Use finishing nails for the smaller pieces, driving the heads below the surface with a nail set *(right)*. The second layer of molding can now be attached the same way as the first.

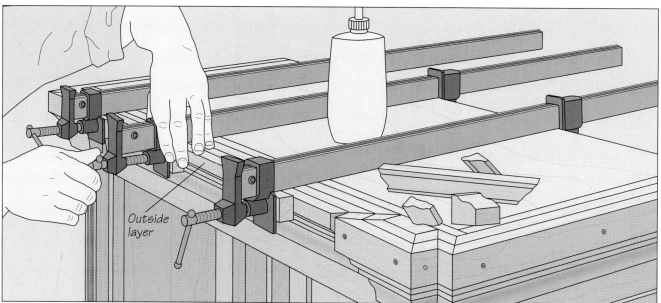

5 Clamping the outside layer of molding in place

Since the outside layer of molding will be entirely visible from the front of the armoire, it should be secured with only glue. As before, apply the sides and main front piece first, then add the small strips around the pilasters. When installing the front piece, spread glue on it and align its top edge with the top of the first two layers of molding. Install three bar clamps across the armoire to secure the piece in place, tightening the clamps gradually in turn until a thin bead of glue squeezes out from the joint; use wood pads to protect the stock *(above)*. If necessary, use cut-off brads *(page 123)* to hold the molding in position while you apply the clamps. Repeat the procedure for the two side pieces. To finish the molding, glue up and install the pieces around the pilasters. Clamp the small front pieces with bar clamps. For the sides, set the pieces in place and install one clamp across the pilaster to secure them both at once.

CUTTING MOLDING ON THE TABLE SAW

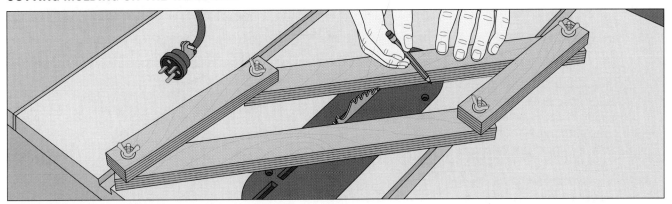

1 Setting the width and marking the guidelines
Fashion cornice molding with the help of the cove-cutting guide shown above. The jig will enable you to cut a cove molding, which can then be ripped in half to produce two cornice moldings. To construct the jig, fasten two 18-inch-long 1-by-2s to two 9-inch-long 1-by-2s with carriage bolts and wing nuts, forming two sets of parallel arms. Adjust the jig so the distance between the inside edges of the two long arms equals twice the width of the coved part of molding you will install. Set the blade height at the desired depth of cut. Lay the guide across the blade and rotate it until the blade, turned by hand, just touches the inside edges of the arms. Then run a pencil along the inside edges of the long arms to trace guidelines on the table insert *(above)*.

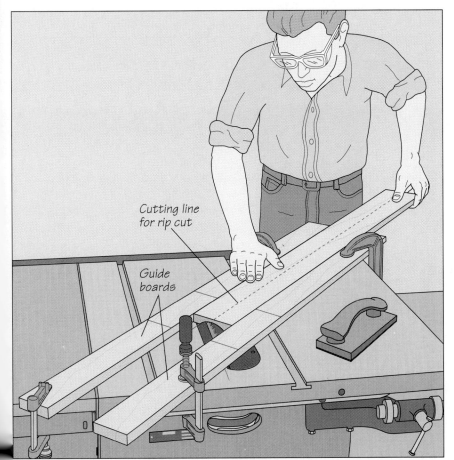

Cutting line
for rip cut

Guide
boards

2 Cutting the cove
Remove the guide and lower the blade beneath the table. Outline the desired cove profile on the leading end of the workpiece, then set the stock on the saw table, aligning the marked outline with the guidelines on the table insert. Butt guide boards against the edges of the workpiece and clamp them parallel to the guidelines; use boards long enough to span the saw table. Draw lines 3 inches to either side of the blade on the guide boards, delineating a danger zone that your hands should avoid. Crank the blade ⅛ inch above the table. To make the first pass, feed the workpiece steadily into the blade with your left hand, while holding the workpiece against the table with your right hand *(left)*. Finish the cut using a push block. Make as many passes as necessary, raising the blade ⅛ inch at a time. For a deep cove, tack a backup board to the top of the workpiece to prevent splitting. For a smooth finish, raise the blade very slightly for the last pass and feed the workpiece slowly into it. When the cut is completed, rip the stock in half to fashion the molding, then sand the pieces.

BUILD IT YOURSELF

MITER JIG

This simple jig will allow you to miter the ends of molding on your radial arm saw with the blade in the normal 90° crosscutting position. Refer to the illustration for suggested dimensions.

To build the jig, bevel the ends of the guides at 45°. Next, cut the base and fence and screw the two pieces together, leaving enough of the fence extending below the base to sit in the slot between the front auxiliary table and the spacer. Then, remove the saw's fence and position the base of the jig on the saw table, seating the fence in the table slot. Set the blade in the 90° crosscutting position and adjust the cutting depth to make a ⅛-inch-deep kerf in the base. Once the cut is made, remove the jig and

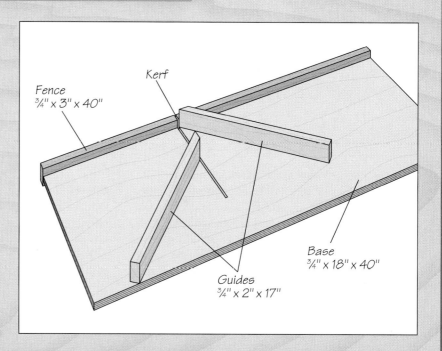

Fence
¾" x 3" x 40"

Kerf

Base
¾" x 18" x 40"

Guides
¾" x 2" x 17"

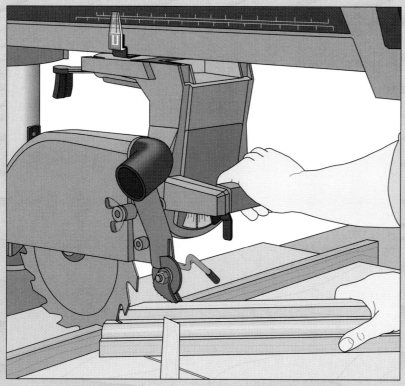

screw one of the guides edge-down on the base with its beveled end flush against the fence and its point just touching the kerf in the base. Position the beveled end of the second guide flush along the kerf in the base. Use a carpenter's square to ensure the second guide is square to the first one, then screw it in place. (There should be enough space between the two guides for the stock you will be cutting.)

Install the jig on the table. Holding the strip of molding firmly against one of the guides, butt the end of the stock against the fence. Turn on the saw and pull the yoke through the cut *(left)*. To cut the mating miter, secure the second piece against the opposite guide, then pull the saw through the cut.

MAKING DENTIL MOLDING

Using a table saw

Dentil molding is a classic ornamental detail consisting of small rectangular blocks, or dentils, with spaces between them. It is made from thin stock, typically between ¼ and ⅜ inch thick, and is placed either directly against the cabinet with another molding on top, or sandwiched between two moldings *(inset)*. First, rip the stock to the desired width. Then install a dado head as wide as the space you want between the dentils, and adjust the blade height to set the length of the blocks. Screw an extension board to the miter gauge, then feed it into the dado head to cut a notch. Move the extension to the right by the width of the dentil, then cut a second notch. Make a small wooden key to fit snugly in the notches; slide it into the first notch until it protrudes about 1 inch. Butt the end of the stock against the key and hold it firmly against the miter gauge to cut the first dentil. For the next cut, place the first notch over the key and repeat the procedure. Continue in this manner until the length of molding is cut *(right)*.

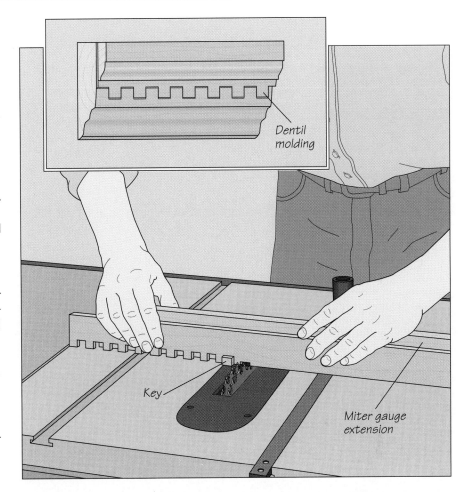

Dentil molding

Key

Miter gauge extension

LEVELING THE ARMOIRE

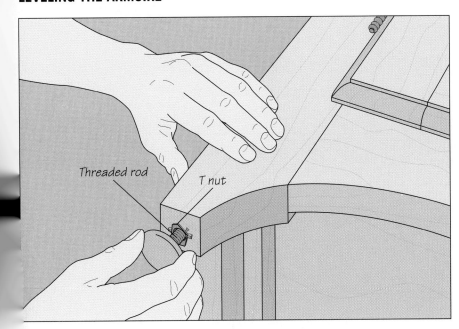

Threaded rod

T nut

Installing adjustable levelers

To compensate for an uneven floor, install adjustable levelers on the base of your armoire. The hardware consists of a T nut and a threaded rod with a plastic foot. Install the levelers by boring holes for the T nuts in the bottom of the feet. Drill them slightly longer than the threaded rods. Tap the nuts into the holes with a mallet, then screw in the levelers *(left)*. Adjust the feet to level the cabinet.

DOORS

The frame-and-panel doors of an armoire are built in much the same way as the side assemblies of a frame-and-panel cabinet *(page 32)*. However, there are differences. Both the inside and outside edges of the stiles and rails can be molded for added decoration. In addition, the mortise-and-tenon joint used to connect the frame pieces incorporates a mitered molding, shown on page 73. A final difference involves the stock used to build doors. Because they swing free, doors have a tendency to deform. To counteract this, doors are often made from heavier stock. To avoid an excessively heavy appearance, the back of the door frame can be rabbeted to allow a portion of the door to remain inside the armoire when it is closed. The resulting lip along the outside edge of each door rests on a vertical mullion dividing the cabinet opening or on a false mullion, which is a strip of wood attached to the edge of the left-hand door.

The glass door shown on page 73 is essentially a frame-and-panel door with glass panels. The glass sits in rabbets cut along the inside edges of the frame and is held in place by strips of molding.

The doors of the armoire above harmonize with the frame-and-panel construction of the piece. Their lip-rabbeted mounting partly recesses the doors into the cabinet, making them appear thin and delicate despite their sturdy construction.

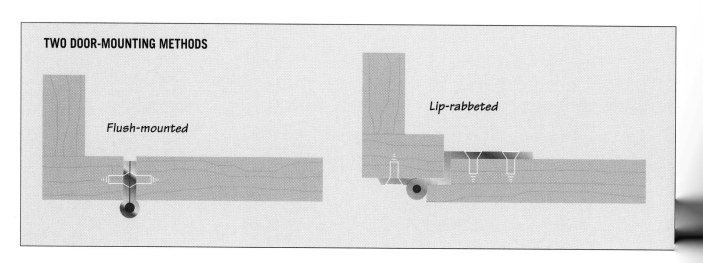

TWO DOOR-MOUNTING METHODS

Flush-mounted

Lip-rabbeted

ARMOIRE

TWO DOOR ANATOMIES

FRAME-AND-PANEL DOOR

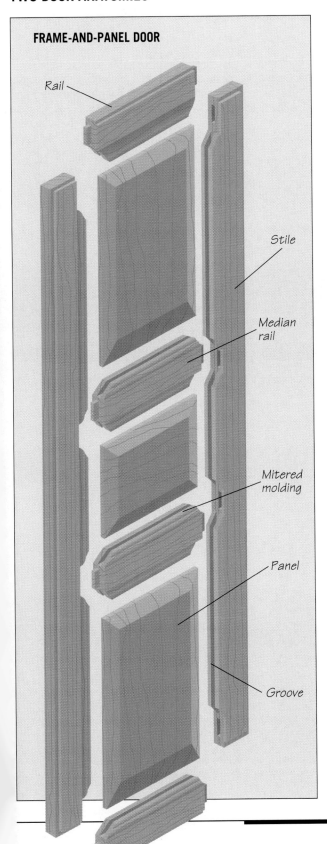

Rail

Stile

Median rail

Mitered molding

Panel

Groove

GLASS DOOR

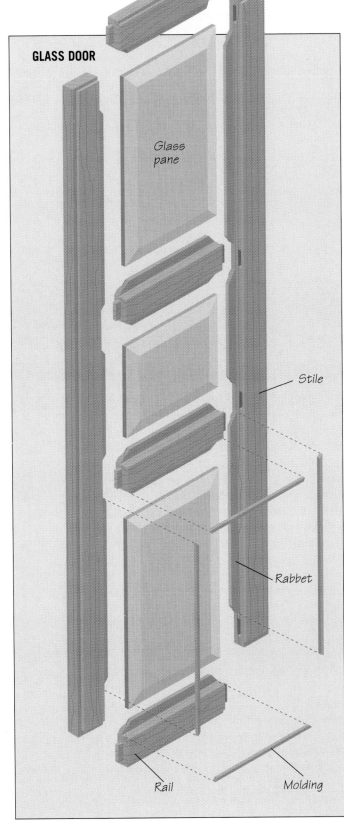

Glass pane

Stile

Rabbet

Rail

Molding

73

MAKING A FRAME-AND-PANEL DOOR

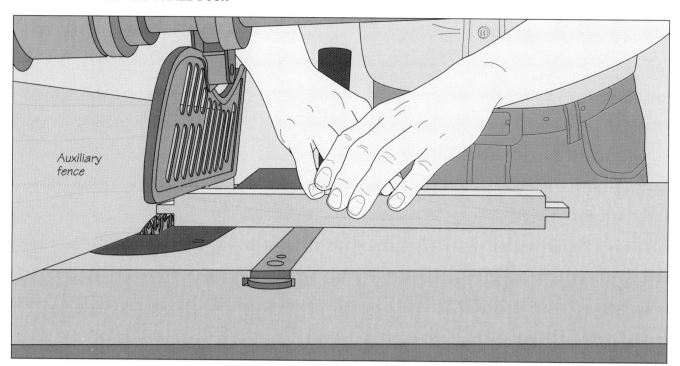

Auxiliary
fence

1 Cutting the tenons

Make your armoire's frame-and-panel doors by cutting blind tenons at the ends of all the rails, as shown here, and then shaping the inside edges of all the frame components, as illustrated in steps 2 through 4. Finally, drill mortises in the stiles *(step 5)* and prepare each frame for a panel *(step 6)*. To cut the tenons on your table saw, install a dado head slightly wider than the tenon length. Install an auxiliary wood fence and notch it by raising the dado head into it. Set the width of cut equal to the tenon length and adjust the cutting height to about one-third the thickness of the stock. Holding the rail flush against the miter gauge and the fence, feed the stock face-down into the blades to cut one tenon cheek. Turn the board over and make the same cut on the other side. Check for fit in a test mortise, then repeat the process on the other end of the board and on the other rails *(above)*. To cut the tenon shoulders, set the cutting height at about ½ inch. Then, with the rail face flush against the miter gauge and the end butted against the fence, feed the workpiece into the blades. Turn the rail over and repeat the cut on the other side *(right)*. Cut the rest of the tenon shoulders the same way.

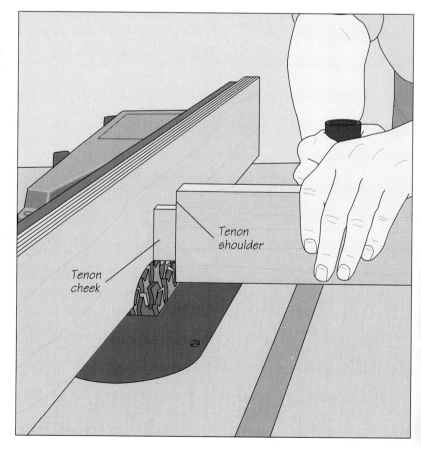

Tenon
shoulder

Tenon
cheek

2 Shaping the rails and stiles

To fashion integrated molding on the inside edges of the door frame, fit your router with a piloted molding bit and mount the tool in a table. Align the fence with the bearing on the bit, then adjust the cutting depth to shape the bottom portion of the board. For each pass, feed the stock good-face-down into the bit, pressing it firmly against the fence; adjust the cutting height, if necessary. Shape only the interior edges of the rails and stiles around the door's perimeter. For a median rail, like the one at right, shape both edges.

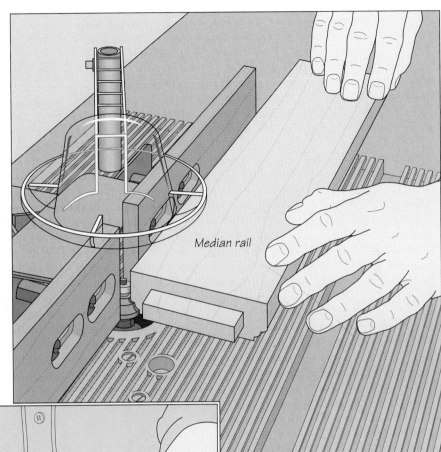

Median rail

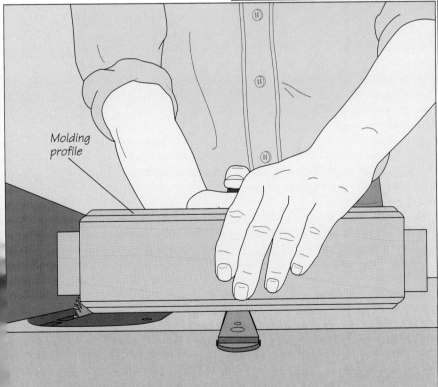

Molding profile

3 Preparing the rails for glue up

The corners of the tenon shoulders must be mitered to mate properly with the stiles. Remove the auxiliary fence from the table saw fence and install a crosscut or combination blade. Set the blade angle to 45°, make a test cut in a scrap board, and check the cut with a combination square. Adjust the fence position and blade height so that the cut is exactly as wide and deep as the width of the edge molding. (The blade teeth should just protrude beyond the tenon shoulder.) To make the cuts, hold the piece flush against the miter gauge and the fence as you feed it edge-down into the blade. Repeat the cuts on the ends of each molded edge of the remaining rails (left).

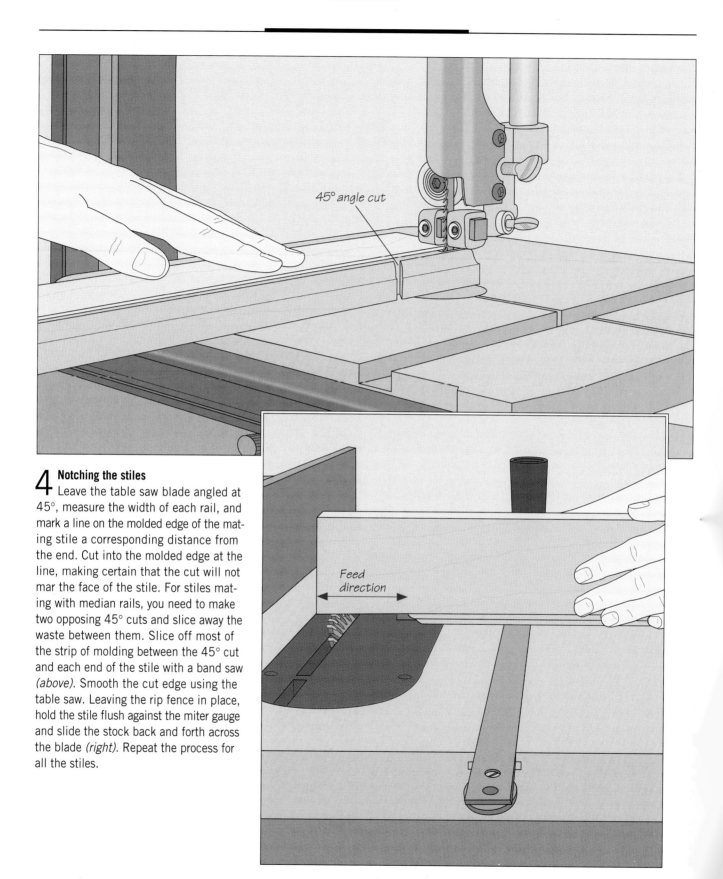

45° angle cut

Feed direction

4 Notching the stiles

Leave the table saw blade angled at 45°, measure the width of each rail, and mark a line on the molded edge of the mating stile a corresponding distance from the end. Cut into the molded edge at the line, making certain that the cut will not mar the face of the stile. For stiles mating with median rails, you need to make two opposing 45° cuts and slice away the waste between them. Slice off most of the strip of molding between the 45° cut and each end of the stile with a band saw *(above)*. Smooth the cut edge using the table saw. Leaving the rip fence in place, hold the stile flush against the miter gauge and slide the stock back and forth across the blade *(right)*. Repeat the process for all the stiles.

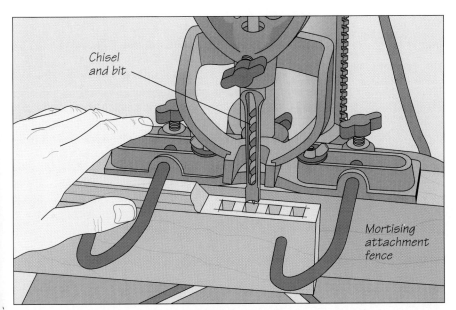

5 Cutting mortises in the stiles

Use one of the tenons you cut in step 1 as a guide to outlining the mortises on the edges of the stiles. To make the job easier, clamp all the stiles together face-to-face with their ends aligned. Install a mortising attachment on your drill press and clamp one stile to the fence, centering the mortise outline under the chisel and bit. Make the drilling depth ⅛ inch more than the tenon length; make a cut at each end of the mortise before boring out the waste in between *(left)*. Repeat the procedure to cut the remaining mortises.

Chisel and bit

Mortising attachment fence

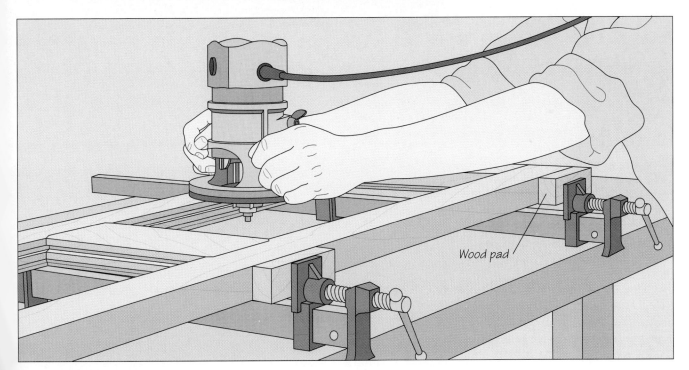

Wood pad

6 Preparing the frames for panels

Cut the panel grooves in the frame edges with your router and a three-wing slotting cutter. Dry-assemble the rails and stiles of each door and clamp the frame face-down on a work table, using wood pads to protect the stock. Adjust the cutting depth of your router to cut a groove midway between the bottom of the frame and the edge of the molding. With a firm grip on the router, lower the base plate onto the surface and guide the bit into the stock near one corner of the frame. Once the bit pilot butts against the edge of the stock, continue the cut in a clockwise direction *(above)*. Repeat the process for the other panel openings. Make a raised panel for each opening *(page 36)* and glue up the door as you would any frame-and-panel assembly. You can now rout a decorative molding around the outside edges of the doors and a rabbet around their back faces; be sure to leave enough stock between the two to install the hinges *(page 79)*.

BUILDING A GLASS DOOR

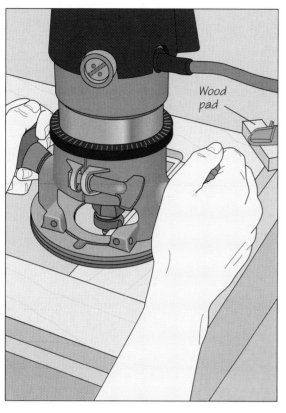

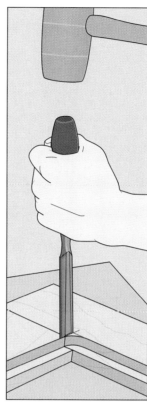

1 Cutting a rabbet to hold glass
Glass panels lie in rabbets rather than grooves and are held in place by thin strips of molding. Clamp the glued-up frame to a work surface, using a wood pad to protect your stock. Then install a ⅜-inch rabbeting bit in a router and set the depth of cut to the combined thickness of the glass and the molding. Hold the tool firmly with both hands while resting the base plate on the frame near one corner, then guide the bit into the inside edge of the door. Move the router clockwise along the edges *(far left)* until the cut is completed. Square the corners with a chisel and a wooden mallet *(near left)*. Make the cuts across the grain first to avoid splitting the frame.

2 Making the molding and gluing up the door
Shape both edges of a board *(page 66)* that is long enough to produce the length of molding you need. Then rip the molding from the stock on a table saw. Cut the molding to length, mitering the ends at 45°. Cut and fit one piece at a time. Once the molding is ready, set a drop of clear glazing compound every few inches to prevent the glass from rattling. Lay the molding in place and, starting 2 inches from the corners, bore pilot holes at 6-inch intervals through the molding and into the frame. Tack down the molding with brads, using a piece of cardboard to protect the glass from the hammer *(right)*.

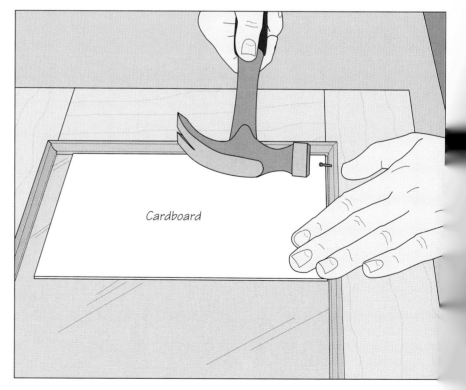

Cardboard

HANGING THE DOORS ON THE ARMOIRE: LACE HINGES

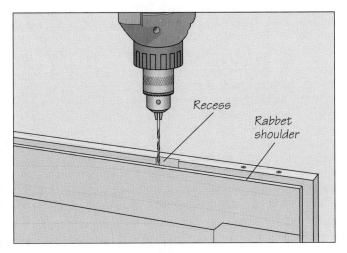

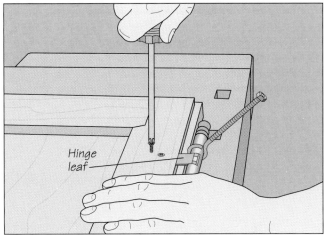

1 Installing the hinges on the doors

The type of hinge shown here attaches to the door with a leaf at each end; bolts fasten the assembly to the armoire. The leaves must be mortised into the door edge. Begin by securing the door edge-up in a vise. Position the hinge on the edge and mark the location of the leaves. At each outline, use a chisel to cut a recess in the cheek of the rabbet around the back of the door equal in depth to the leaf thickness; stop the cut at the rabbet shoulder. Then fit an electric drill with a twist bit equal in diameter to the thickness of the leaf and bore a series of overlapping holes to extend the recesses down into the shoulder *(above, left)*. Periodically test-fit the leaves in the mortises, tapping them in with a mallet; stop drilling once the hinge rests flush on the edge of the door with the leaves in their mortises. Remove the hinge from the door, lay the door flat on a work surface and position the hinge on the edge, leaving the leaves outside the mortises. Mark screw holes on the back face of the door stile and bore a countersunk hole at each mark. Slide the hinge leaves back into the mortises, and drive the screws to secure the hinge to the door *(above, right)*.

2 Installing the door

To mount the hinge bolts to the armoire, set the piece on its back. Working with a helper, if necessary, hold the door in position and mark the bolt locations on the front stile of the armoire. Bore a clearance hole at each mark, then reposition the door on the piece, slipping the bolts into the holes *(left)*. Fix the door in place with the nuts provided.

HANGING THE DOORS: CLOCK-CASE HINGES

1 Positioning the hinges
Set the armoire on its back. For each door, fix strips of masking tape across the corners of the opening. Place small sandpaper shims beside the pieces of tape to prevent the door from inadvertently shifting as you work. Set the door in place, centering it over the opening. Measure from both sides to make certain the door is parallel to the stiles. Once you are satisfied with the positioning, mark the corners of the door on the tape with a pencil. Next, butt the hinges against the edge of the door; use a tape measure to make sure that they are equally spaced from the top and bottom of the door *(right)*. Holding the upper half of the hinge in place, slip off the bottom half and the hinge pin and use a pencil to mark the screw holes on the door edge *(below)*.

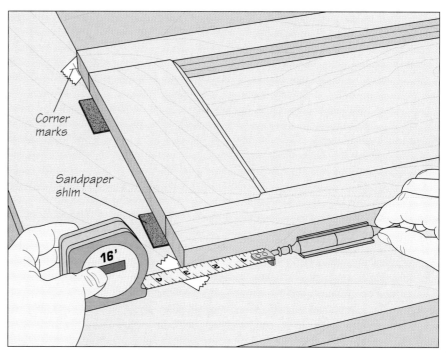

Corner marks

Sandpaper shim

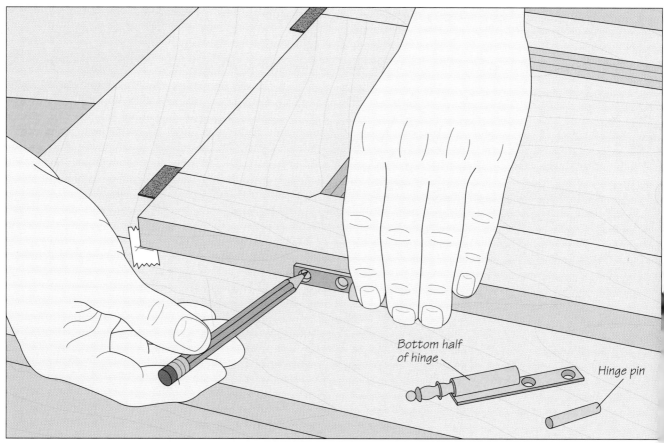

Bottom half of hinge

Hinge pin

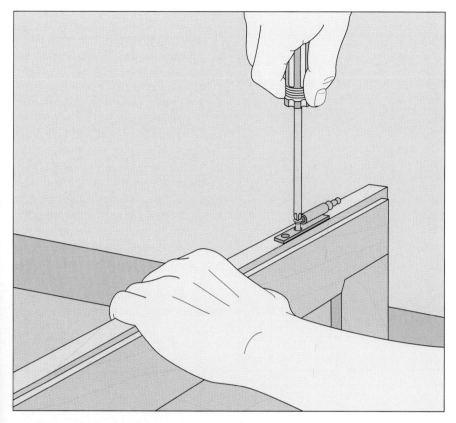

2 Mounting the hinges on the door

Secure the door edge-up on a work surface, then bore pilot holes at each marked point. Hold the top half of each hinge square to the door edge and screw it in place *(left)*.

3 Hanging the door

Place the door back on the armoire and reassemble the hinges. Check that the corners of the door are aligned with the marks on the masking tape. Trace around the bottom of the hinges with a pencil, remove the door, disassemble the hinges, and reposition the bottom halves on the armoire. Mark the screw holes on the cabinet, bore pilot holes, and screw the bottom half of each hinge to the armoire *(below)*. Remove the shims and tape strips, insert the pin in the bottom half of the hinge, and place the door on the armoire.

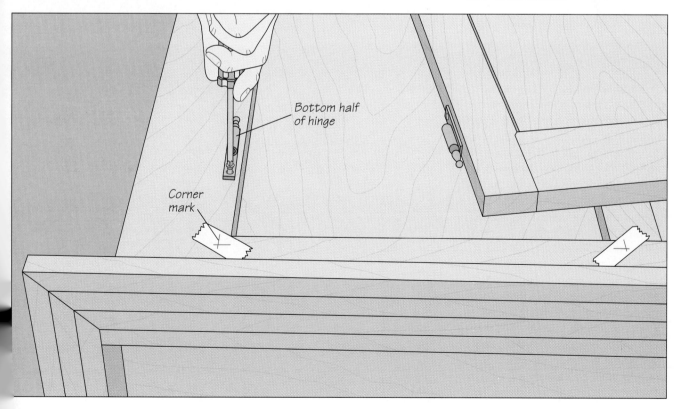

Bottom half of hinge

Corner mark

HANGING THE DOORS: RAT-TAIL HINGES

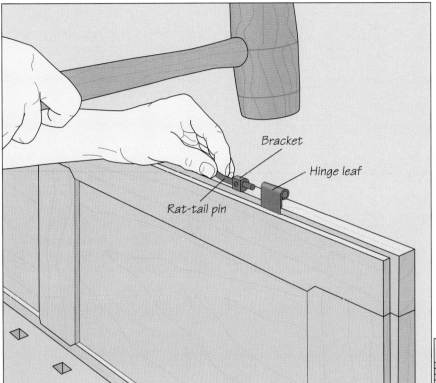

Bracket

Hinge leaf

Rat-tail pin

1 Mounting the hinges on the door
Measure the distance between the top edge of the hinge leaf and the screw holes in the leaf; the holes will be hidden once the leaf is ready to be fastened to the door. Make a mortise for each hinge leaf as you would for lace hinges *(page 79)*. With the door edge-up in a vise, slide the leaf into its mortise. Then slip the rat-tail pin into its bracket and set the bracket on the door edge with the tail pointing toward the bottom of the door. Holding the pin and bracket in position, tap the leaf deeper into the door edge until the hole in the leaf aligns with the pin *(left)*. Measure from the top of the leaf to mark its screw holes on the door and bore countersunk holes. Drive the screws to fix the leaf to the door.

2 Mounting the door
Position the door in its opening in the armoire and assemble the hinge, sliding the rat-tail pin into the hole in the leaf. Fastening the hinge to the armoire is a two-step operation, beginning with the bracket. Trace its outline on the armoire, remove the bracket and pin, then bore a clearance hole for the bracket bolt supplied with the hinge through the center of the outline. Thread the bolt into the bracket, slip the bolt into the clearance hole, and use the nut supplied to fasten the bracket to the armoire. Then slide the pin into the bracket, checking that the rat-tail lies flat on the cabinet; bend the tail in a vise, if necessary, to make it sit flat. Reassemble the hinge one final time and use a finishing nail to fasten the rat-tail to the armoire *(right)*.

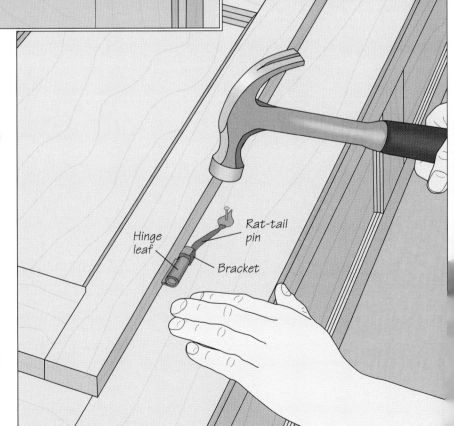

Hinge leaf

Rat-tail pin

Bracket

INSTALLING A LOCK

1 Cutting the keyhole

To mark the keyhole location on the door, measure the distance between the outside edge of the lock and the center of the key chamber on the inside of the lock. (The lock being installed here is illustrated on page 63.) Then transfer your measurement to the door, measuring from the rabbet cheek on the door's back face. You need to drill two holes for the key: one for the shaft and a narrower one for the key bit, which is the strip of metal below the forward end of the shaft. Bore the wider hole first, using an electric drill fitted with a twist bit slightly larger than the key shaft. Then fit the drill with a bit slightly larger than the thickness of the key bit and bore a second hole below the shaft hole *(right)*; locate the hole to suit the key. Hold the door steady as you drill the holes. Use a small file or a riffler to join the two holes and create a cavity through which the key fits easily.

Hole for key shaft

2 Mounting the lock and making the bolt mortise

Position the lock on the back of the door, sliding the key chamber in the hole in the door, and fit the key into the lock. With the key in place, hold the lock steady while fastening it to the door *(left)*. Make sure that the lock is square to the edge of the door as you drive the screws. To locate the mortise for the bolt, turn the key to extend the bolt and use a pencil to coat the end of the bolt with graphite. Retract the bolt and close the door. Extend the bolt against the edge of the mullion to mark its location and use the drill and a chisel to cut a mortise centered on the pencil mark. If desired, install an escutcheon around the keyhole.

Bolt

Rabbet cheek

Key

BLANKET CHEST

The chest is one of the earliest types of furniture, with a long utilitarian tradition. During the Middle Ages, chests served as the primary receptacles of household goods and valuables. They were also called upon to perform double duty as a seating place, at a time when chairs were a luxury for most people.

Although early chest designs were primitive, medieval artisans often adorned them with carved arches and elaborate chivalric and battle scenes. During the Renaissance and Baroque periods, the piece began to assume some of the elements that are still used today, including frame-and-panel joinery, molded tops and bases, and patterned bracket feet. Over the years, attractive hardware was added, such as brass locks, handles, and escutcheons.

In Colonial America, the chest was usually placed at the foot of a bed to store blankets, quilts, and linens—hence the name blanket chest. Today, the piece is used to store everything from toys and clothing to books. Many chests are built with drawers for additional storage.

A biscuit joiner cuts a slot in the mitered end of the blanket chest's molded base. The base is rabbeted to accept the carcase of the chest and the bracket feet are then screwed to the base.

Blanket chests are all relatively similar, beginning with a rectangular carcase and a hinged top. Dimensions vary, but as a general guideline consider a length of 40 to 45 inches, a width of 18 to 20 inches, and a height of about 25 inches. The carcase is made from panels of edge-glued boards and assembled with dovetail or frame-and-panel joinery. The top features routed wood strips that are attached with sliding dovetail joints *(page 91);* or a molding can be cut into its edge *(page 92)*. To prevent the top from warping, and as a decorative touch, wood battens can be fastened for stiffening *(page 92)*. The top can be attached with a piano hinge *(page 88)* or butt hinges *(page 89)*.

The techniques for making base molding and bracket feet for a blanket chest are discussed starting on page 93. You might choose instead to install ogee bracket feet; these make a fitting base for bookcases and armoires as well. Installing blanket box hardware is shown starting on page 100. These items provide the final decorative touch and should be chosen carefully to complement the particular design of your project.

This traditional dovetailed chest, with its patterned feet and molded top and bottom, is based on a design imported to America from eastern Europe in the 18th Century.

ANATOMY OF A BLANKET CHEST

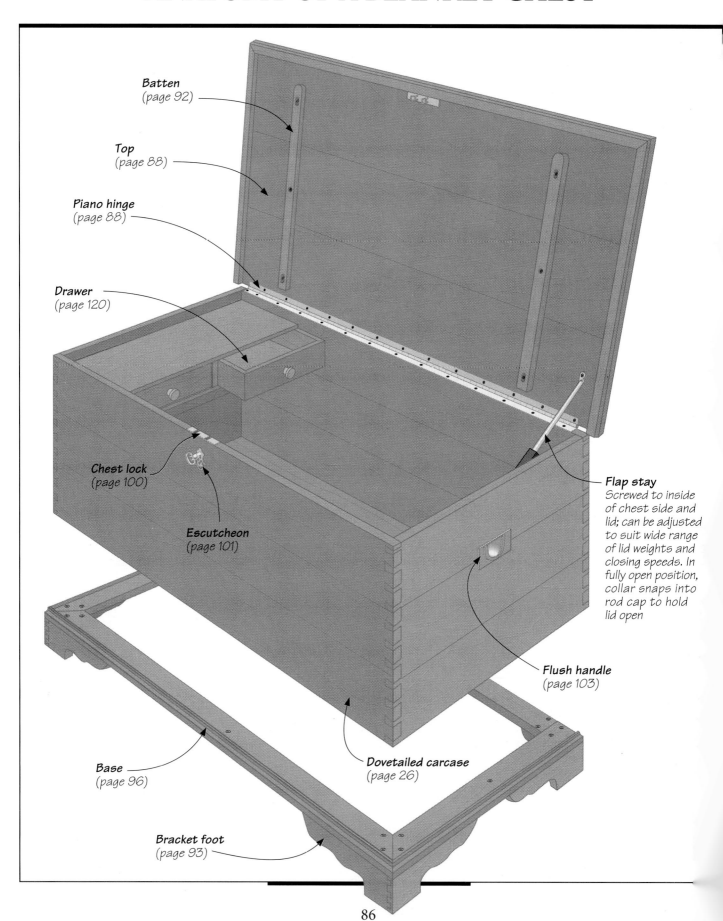

Batten
(page 92)

Top
(page 88)

Piano hinge
(page 88)

Drawer
(page 120)

Chest lock
(page 100)

Escutcheon
(page 101)

Flap stay
Screwed to inside of chest side and lid; can be adjusted to suit wide range of lid weights and closing speeds. In fully open position, collar snaps into rod cap to hold lid open

Flush handle
(page 103)

Dovetailed carcase
(page 26)

Base
(page 96)

Bracket foot
(page 93)

Traditional blanket chests were often furnished with one or more drawers to store anything from papers and pens to sewing needles and thread. The top and bottom panels of the drawer assembly are mounted in stopped grooves in the front and back panels of the chest, with a divider to separate the opening for the drawers.

INVENTORY OF BLANKET CHEST HARDWARE

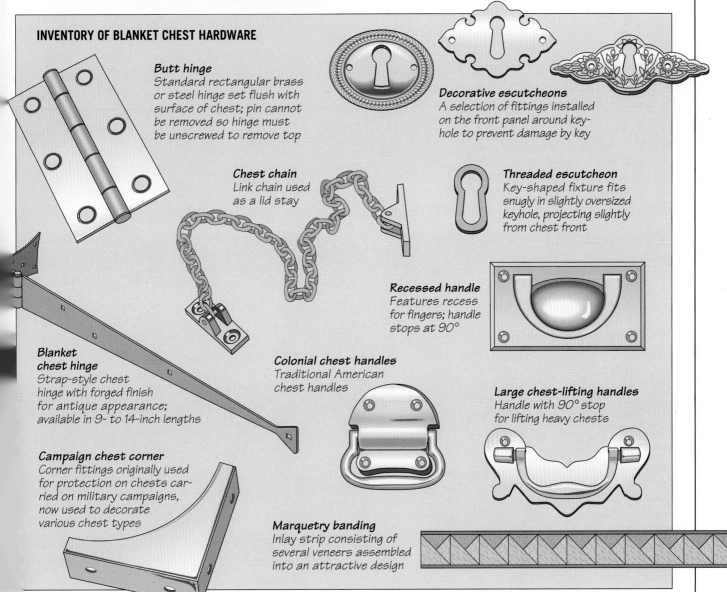

Butt hinge
Standard rectangular brass or steel hinge set flush with surface of chest; pin cannot be removed so hinge must be unscrewed to remove top

Decorative escutcheons
A selection of fittings installed on the front panel around keyhole to prevent damage by key

Chest chain
Link chain used as a lid stay

Threaded escutcheon
Key-shaped fixture fits snugly in slightly oversized keyhole, projecting slightly from chest front

Recessed handle
Features recess for fingers; handle stops at 90°

Blanket chest hinge
Strap-style chest hinge with forged finish for antique appearance; available in 9- to 14-inch lengths

Colonial chest handles
Traditional American chest handles

Large chest-lifting handles
Handle with 90° stop for lifting heavy chests

Campaign chest corner
Corner fittings originally used for protection on chests carried on military campaigns, now used to decorate various chest types

Marquetry banding
Inlay strip consisting of several veneers assembled into an attractive design

Since molding strips are fastened around its edges with sliding dovetails to accommodate wood movement, the chest top shown at left does not require battens to keep it flat, though two have been added for decorative effect. The lid stay holds the top open and allows it to close slowly to avoid damaging the piece.

ATTACHING THE TOP WITH A PIANO HINGE

Installing the hinge

The hinge should be equal to or slightly shorter than the length of the chest. Clamp the top to a work surface using wood pads to protect the stock. Hold the hinge in position, aligning the center of the pin with the back edge of the top, and trace its outline. Next, install a straight bit in a router and set the cutting depth to the thickness of the hinge leaf. (Take care adjusting the depth; if the rabbet is too deep it will cause the hinge to bind when the lid is closed.) Align the bit over the inside edge of the outline, then fasten an edge guide butted against the router base plate. Rout the inside edge of the rabbet, keeping the base plate pressed against the edge guide. Make repeat cuts, adjusting the edge guide each time, until the rabbet is completed. Then, set the hinge in the rabbet and mark the location of the screw holes. If you are adding molding *(page 91)* or battens *(page 92)*, do so now. Then bore pilot holes at the marks, put the hinge back in position *(right),* and drive the screws. Set the top on the chest, with the free hinge leaf flat on the top edge of the blanket chest's back panel. Mark the location for the screws, bore pilot holes, and drive in the screws.

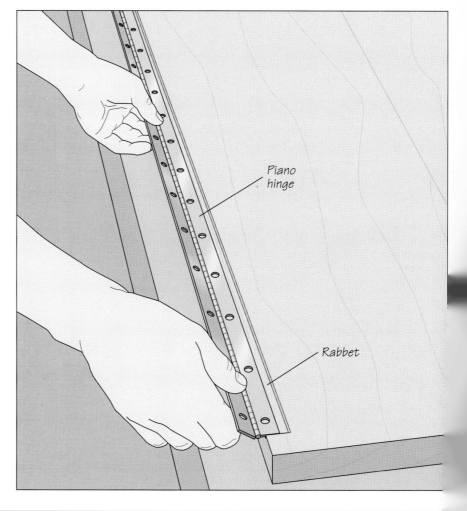

Piano hinge

Rabbet

ATTACHING THE TOP WITH BUTT HINGES

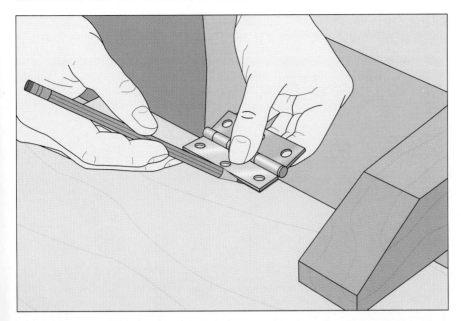

1 Tracing the hinge outlines
Instead of a piano hinge, you can use two or three butt hinges to attach the top to the blanket chest. The hinges are mortised into both the top and back panel of the chest. To begin, clamp the top good-side down on a work surface and place the first hinge in position a few inches in from one end, positioning the pin just off the back edge of the top. Use a pencil to trace the outline of the hinge *(left)*. Mark the other hinges on the top in the same manner, positioning one near the other end and one in the center, if necessary.

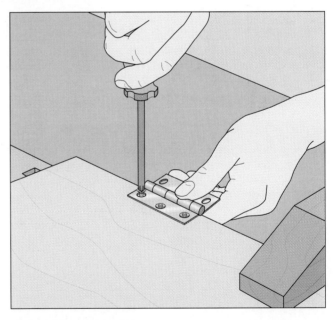

2 Chiseling out the waste
Use a chisel to score the hinge outline and cut it to the thickness of the hinge. Then, holding the chisel bevel up, pare the waste from the mortise *(above)*. Repeat the procedure to clear out the remaining mortises. Be careful to cut the mortises no deeper than the thickness of the hinge leaves to prevent binding.

3 Installing the hinges
Set the hinges in their mortises in the top, drill pilot holes, and screw them in place *(above)*. Next, set the top on the chest, mark the location for the corresponding hinge mortises on the top edge of the back panel, then chisel them out following the procedure described in step 2. Now lay the chest on its back on a work surface and set the top good-face down behind it. Place a wood spacer slightly thicker than the top under the back of the blanket chest to line-up the free hinge leaves with their mortises. Bore pilot holes and screw the hinges in place.

HINGE MORTISING JIG

A router is an ideal tool to cut mortises for your blanket chest's butt hinges, but do not try to do the job freehand. A jig like the one shown at right will guarantee fast, accurate results. You will need to equip your router with a straight bit and a template guide to make the cuts.

Make the template from a piece of ¾-inch plywood wide enough to support the router. Outline the hinge leaf on the template, being sure to compensate for the template guide and the thickness of the fence, which is also made from ¾-inch plywood. Cut out the template, then attach the fence with countersunk screws.

To use the jig, secure the top of the chest edge-up in a vise. Mark the hinge outline on the workpiece and clamp the template in position, aligning the cutout with the outline

on the edge and butting the fence against the inner face of the top. Make the cut *(below)*, moving the router in small clockwise circles until the bottom of the recess is smooth, then

square the corners with a chisel. When you are using the jig to cut mortises in the top edge of the blanket chest, be sure to secure the carcase to prevent it from moving.

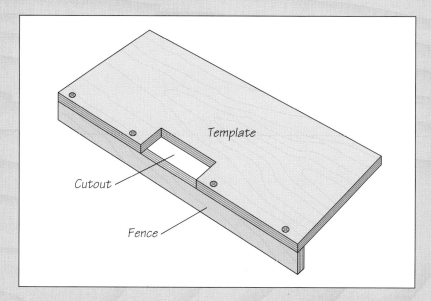

Template

Cutout

Fence

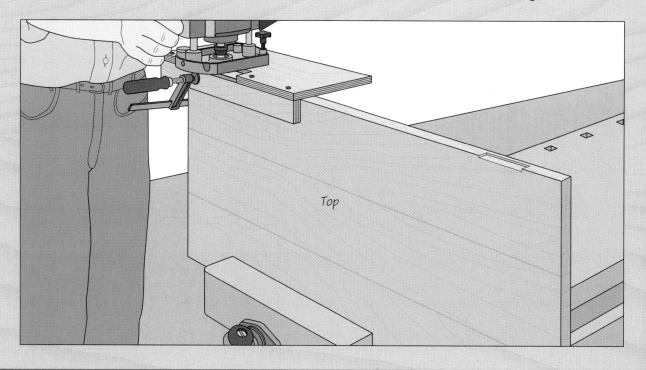

Top

ADDING MOLDING TO THE TOP

1 Making the molding
Install a molding bit in a router and mount the tool in a table. Rout the molding from stock thicker than the top so that when the lid is shut the molding will overhang the side and front panels slightly. (The stock should also be wider and longer than you need so that you can rip and crosscut the molding to size later.) Align the fence with the bearing and feed the board into the bit to carve the design in one half of an edge. Mount a featherboard on either side of the bit to secure the piece during the cut. (In the illustration, the front featherboard has been removed for clarity.) Flip the piece over and rout the other half, creating a mirror cut of the first *(right)*. Then rip and crosscut the molding to the size you need.

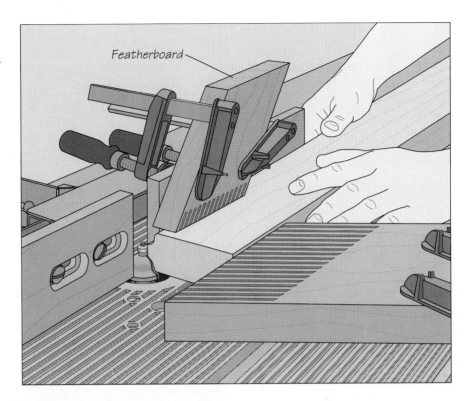

Featherboard

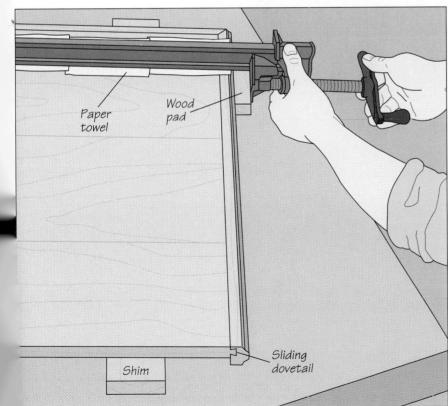

Paper towel

Wood pad

Shim

Sliding dovetail

2 Installing the molding
You can secure the molding to the edge with sliding dovetails or glue alone. In this case, the side moldings are attached with stopped sliding dovetails to allow for cross-grain wood movement; the front molding, which will shrink and swell parallel to the top panel, is attached with glue. Make stopped dovetails on the ends of the top; cut stopped dovetail mortises in the side moldings *(see page 127)*. After you have made the dovetail joints, miter the ends of the molding at 45°. Then place the top good-face up on wood shims. Spread a thin layer of glue on the last two inches of the sliding dovetail and the dovetail slot, then slide the molding into position. Next, lay some paper towel on the top to prevent scratches and install bar clamps with protective wood pads to secure the molding in place *(left)*.

ROUTING MOLDING IN THE TOP

Top

1 Routing the edge
Instead of attaching separate strips of molding, you can rout a decorative shape in the top itself. Secure the top good-face up on a work surface with its edge projecting off the surface. Install a piloted rounding-over bit or another molding bit in your router, then set the cutting height to mold the top part of the edge. Turn on the tool and guide the bit into the stock, moving the tool against the direction of bit rotation and keeping the pilot bearing butted against the stock *(left)*. Once the top half of the edge is molded, flip the workpiece over and rout the bottom half if called for by your design.

2 Adding battens
When molding is attached with sliding dovetails, it serves to stiffen the top, eliminating the need for battens; molding that is simply routed in the edge of the top does not offer this advantage. In this case, to prevent warping from changing humidity levels, fasten two or three battens across the underside of the top. Cut the strips of wood from the same stock as the top, making them about 1½ inches wide and 3 inches shorter than the width of the top. For visual appeal, round one end of each batten on the band saw. Next, set the top good-face down on a work surface and hold the first batten in place about 5 inches from one end of the top. Drive three screws to fasten it in place *(right)*. (To allow the batten to expand and contract, enlarge the counterbored holes at the ends of the wood strips into ovals; the center screw is the only one that should be driven in tight.) Repeat the process to mount the other battens.

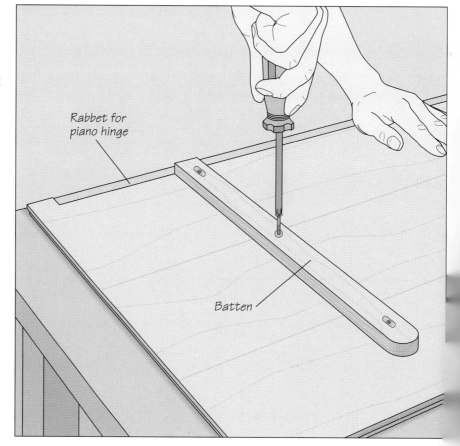

Rabbet for
piano hinge

Batten

BASES AND FEET

The bottom assembly of the blanket chest consists of bracket feet mounted with screws to a rabbeted base molding that supports the carcase. The bracket feet are joined with half-blind dovetails.

MAKING BRACKET FEET

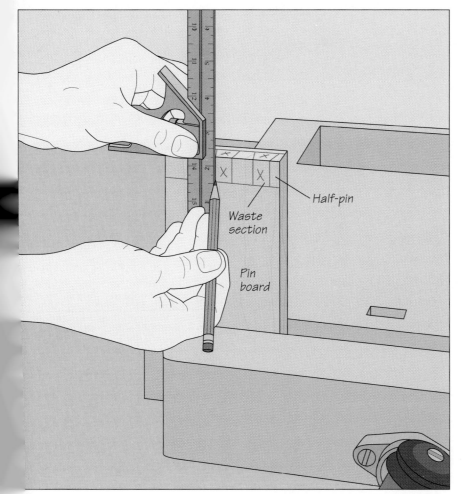

Half-pin

Waste section

Pin board

1 Marking the pin board

The feet of the blanket chest are made from two identical boards cut with a decorative scroll pattern and joined with half-blind dovetail joints. Make the joinery cuts first, then saw out the patterns and assemble the pieces. To begin, cut blanks to the size of the feet, then mark the half-blind dovetails. Indicate the outside face of each board with an X. Then adjust a cutting gauge to the thickness of the stock and scribe a line across the inside face of the pin board to mark the shoulder line. Next, secure the board end-up in a vise, set the cutting gauge to about one-third the stock's thickness, and mark a line across the end closer to its outside face. Use a dovetail square to mark the pins on the end of the board. For the size of board shown, a half-pin at each edge and two evenly spaced pins in between will make a strong and attractive joint. Indicate the waste sections with Xs, then use a combination square to extend the lines down the inside face to the shoulder line *(left)*. Repeat the marks on all the pin boards.

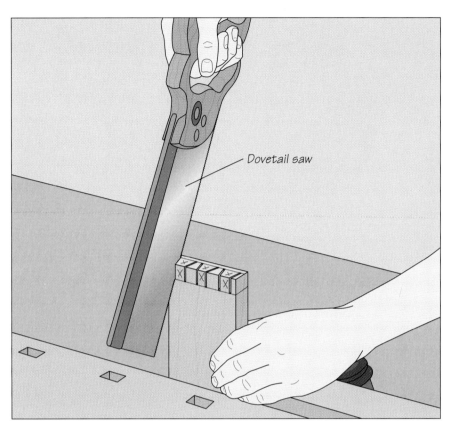

Dovetail saw

2 Cutting the pins

Secure a pin board in a vise with its outside face toward you, then cut down along the edges of the pins with a dovetail saw, working from one edge of the board to the other. For each cut, align the saw blade just to the waste side of the cutting lines *(left)*. Use smooth, even strokes, continuing the cuts to the shoulder line. Next, clamp the board outside-face down on a work surface and use a chisel and mallet to pare away the waste wood: Score a line about ⅛ inch deep along the shoulder line and then shave off a thin layer of waste, with the chisel held horizontally and bevel-up. Repeat the procedure to cut the remaining pin boards.

3 Cutting the tails

Set a cutting gauge to the thickness of the pins, then mark the shoulder line on all the tail boards. Place the first tail board outside-face down on the work surface. Hold a pin board end-down with its inside face aligned with the shoulder line of the tail board, making certain the edges of the boards are flush. Outline the tails with a pencil, then use a try square to extend the lines onto the end of the board. Mark all the waste sections with Xs. Then use a dovetail saw to cut the tails *(right)*. Angling the board, rather than the saw, makes for easier cutting. Then secure the board edge-up in the vise and cut the waste beside the two outside tails. Remove the waste between the tails with a chisel using the same technique described in step 2. When you have chiseled out half the waste, flip the piece and finish the job from the other side. Repeat the process to cut the other tail boards.

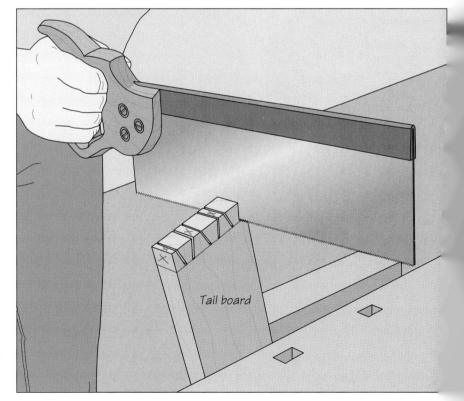

Tail board

4 Test-fitting the joint

Make a template with the desired pattern for the feet and trace the shape on one face of each board. Then, test-fit the half-blind dovetail joint *(right)*. Mark any spots that bind with a pencil and carefully pare some wood away at each mark until the fit is satisfactory.

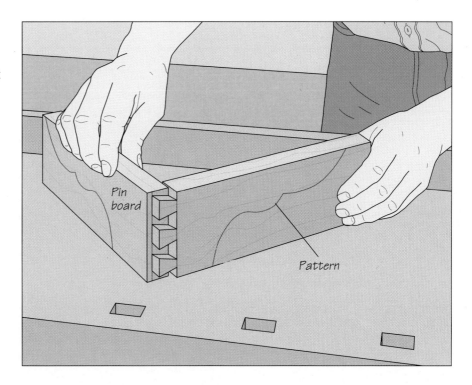

Pin board

Pattern

CUTTING THE PATTERN

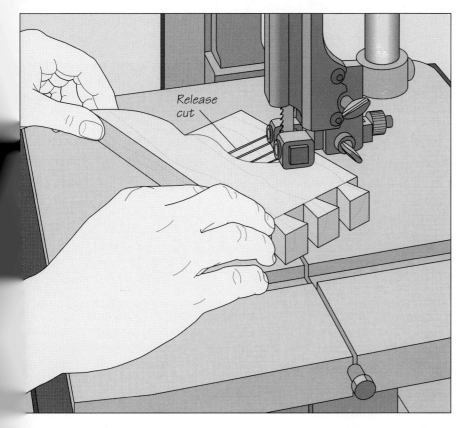

Release cut

Using the band saw

Cut the pattern in each of the feet free-hand on the band saw. To keep the blade from binding in the kerf at the tight part of the curve, make a series of straight release cuts from the edge of the work-piece to the marked line. Then, align the blade just to the waste side of the cutting line and feed the workpiece into the blade with both hands, making sure neither hand is in line with the cutting edge *(left)*.

MAKING THE BASE MOLDING

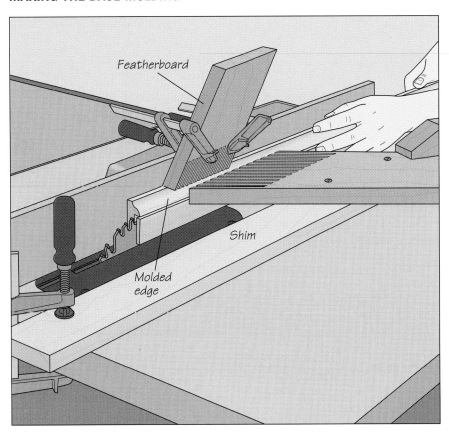

1 Making the base pieces
The four pieces that make up the base molding are shaped and rabbeted individually. Working with stock longer than you need, rout one edge of the front and side pieces the same way you would shape cornice molding *(page 66)*. Next use your table saw to cut rabbets in all four pieces. The rabbets are sawn in two passes, with the shoulders first, followed by the cheeks. Adjust the blade height so the cheeks will be wide enough to support the chest without reaching the molding cuts; position the fence so one-third of the stock thickness will be cut away. Use two featherboards to support the workpiece; attach the table-mounted featherboard a shim so the middle of the workpiece is pressed against the fence. Feed each piece on edge into the blade *(left)* until the trailing end reaches the table. Then move to the other side of the table and pull the stock past the blade.

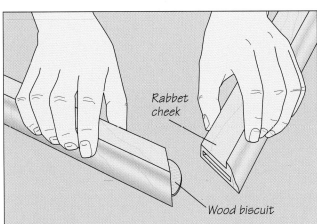

2 Gluing up the base
Saw the molding pieces to length, cutting miters at both ends of the front piece and at one end of the sides. The front corners of the base are assembled with miter joints; butt joints are sufficient for the back. The connections should be reinforced with wood biscuits. Use a plate joiner to cut slots, then spread glue in the slots, insert biscuits in the front and back pieces, and press the corners together *(above)* and clamp them.

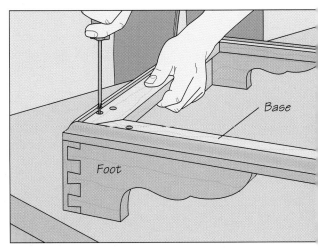

3 Fastening the feet to the base
Working on a flat surface, position the base on the feet of the chest, making sure all the outer edges are flush. At each corner, bore four countersunk holes through the base and into the foot and screw the two together *(above)*. Place the chest in the rabbets of the base piece and drive screws from underneath through the base and into the chest.

A VARIATION: OGEE BRACKET FEET

It is easier to sand the contoured surfaces of the ogee bracket feet before installing them on the base.

MAKING OGEE BRACKET FEET

1 Cutting the ogee cove
Ogee bracket feet are created much like the bracket feet shown on page 93, but with an S-shaped ogee profile shaped in their outside faces. Because of their contoured surfaces, the two halves of each foot are joined with a miter-and-spline joint *(page 98)*, rather than a half-blind dovetail. The ogee profile is cut in three steps on the table saw and the router. Begin by marking the profile on the end of a piece of stock long enough to make all the feet. Set up your table saw to make a cove cut in the face of the board as you would for the cornice molding of an armoire *(page 69)*. Use a push block to feed the stock, making several shallow passes to cut a cove of the appropriate depth *(right)*. Once you have made the cove cut, use a router fitted with a rounding-over bit to shape the corner of the board to the marked line.

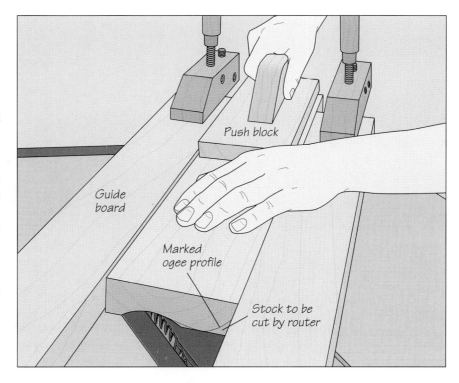

Push block

Guide board

Marked ogee profile

Stock to be cut by router

2 Finishing the ogee profile

The ridge of waste between the cove cut and the rounding-over cut is sliced off by the table saw. To set up the cut, hold the workpiece on edge on the saw table and adjust the blade angle to align the cutting edge with the marked line on the board end. Butt the rip fence against the stock, lock it in place, and set the blade height to slice away the waste. Use three featherboards to support the workpiece during the cut: Clamp two to the fence and a third to the table; this featherboard should be mounted on a shim so it will press closer to the middle of the stock against the fence. Feed the workpiece with both hands *(right)*. Once the board's trailing end reaches the table, move to the other side of the table and pull the stock past the blade.

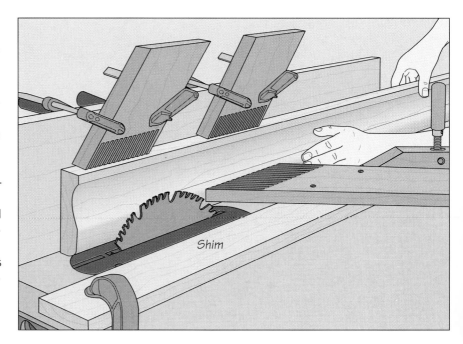

Shim

ASSEMBLING OGEE BRACKET FEET

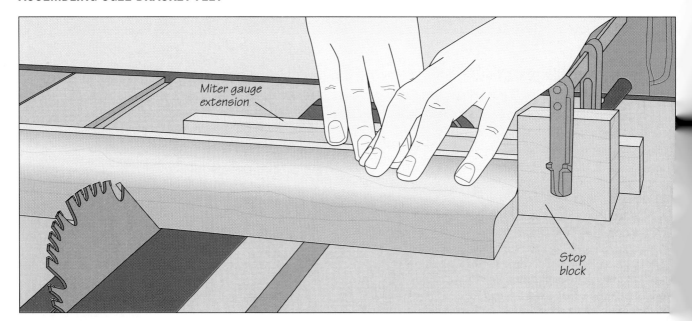

Miter gauge extension

Stop block

1 Making the bevel cuts

Since the ogee bracket feet will be assembled with miter-and-spline joints, each of the eight foot pieces will have bevels on adjoining ends. First, cut all the pieces slightly oversize. To cut the bevels, set your saw's blade angle to 45° and attach a wood extension to the miter gauge. Mark the length of a foot piece on your stock and, holding the flat edge of the board against the extension, align the mark with the blade.

Before making the cut, clamp a stop block to the extension to enable you to line up the cuts for the three other identical pieces. Hold the flat edge of the board against the extension and the end against the block as you make each cut *(above)*. To bevel the ends of the four matching foot pieces, hold the contoured edge of the stock against the extension as you make the cuts.

2 Cutting the spline grooves

The grooves for the splines in the beveled ends of the foot pieces are cut on the table saw. Install a dado head and adjust its thickness to that of the splines you will use. Set the angle of the head at 45° and shift the rip fence to the left-hand side of the blades. Holding one foot piece flat-face-down on the saw table, butt the beveled end against the cutting edges of the dado head and adjust the fence and blade height so a ⅜-inch groove will be located about ¼ inch from the bottom of the piece. Butt the fence against the end of the stock and lock it in place. Feed each piece with the miter gauge *(left)*, pressing the end against the fence throughout the cut.

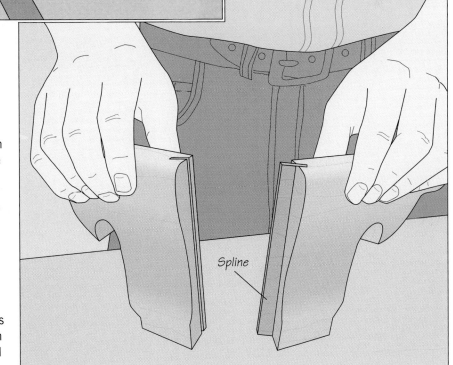

Spline

3 Cutting the patterns and gluing up the feet

Once all the spline grooves are cut, design the scroll patterns on the flat faces of the pieces and cut them out on the band saw *(page 95)*. Sand the pieces smooth, then cut splines from plywood or solid wood to fit into the grooves. The splines should be as long as the grooves; make their width slightly less than twice the combined depth of two grooves. (If you use solid wood for the splines, cut them so the grain runs across their width, rather than lengthwise.) Spread adhesive in the grooves and glue up the feet *(right)*, then attach them to the base as you would standard bracket feet *(page 96)*.

HARDWARE

INSTALLING A LOCK

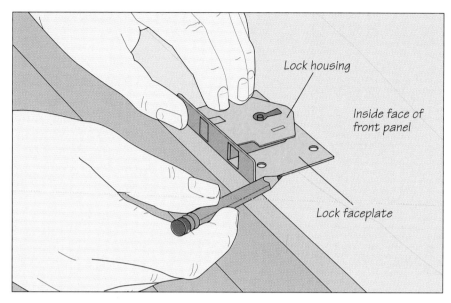

A common feature of traditional campaign chests, solid brass flush handles add a touch of class to any blanket chest. The handles stop at a 90° angle to the sides of the chest, providing a convenient way to lift the piece.

1 Outlining the lock faceplate
Lay the chest on its front panel and position the lock face-down midway between the sides and flush with the top edge of the panel. Trace the outline of the faceplate *(above)*, then extend the lines onto the top edge of the panel.

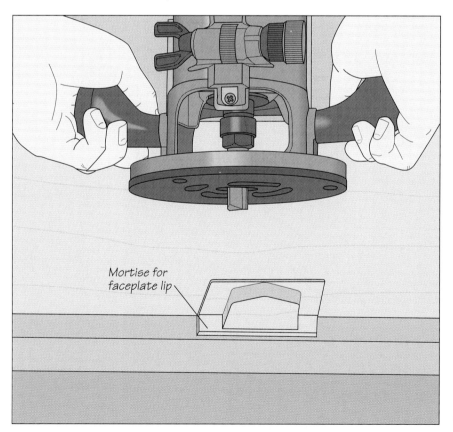

2 Routing the lock mortise
This is one of the rare instances in which the router is used to make a free-hand cut. Care and patience are required. Use a wood chisel to first cut a shallow mortise for the faceplate lip in the top edge of the front panel. Next, install a straight bit in your router, set the cutting depth to the thickness of the faceplate, and cut a mortise inside the marked outline. Start by guiding the tool in a clockwise direction to cut the outside edges of the mortise; clear out the remaining waste by feeding the tool against the direction of bit rotation. Use the chisel to square the corners and pare to the line. Measure the distance between the edges of the faceplate and the lock housing and transfer the measurement to the mortise. Adjust the router's cutting depth to the thickness of the housing and cut the final mortise *(left)*. Use the chisel to square any corners. Test-fit the lock in the cavity and use the chisel to deepen or widen any of the mortises, if necessary.

3 Cutting the keyhole

Set the lock in the mortise and mark the location of the keyhole. Cut the opening as you would for an armoire lock *(page 83)*, drilling one hole for the key shaft and another for the key bit. Use a small file to join the two holes *(right)*.

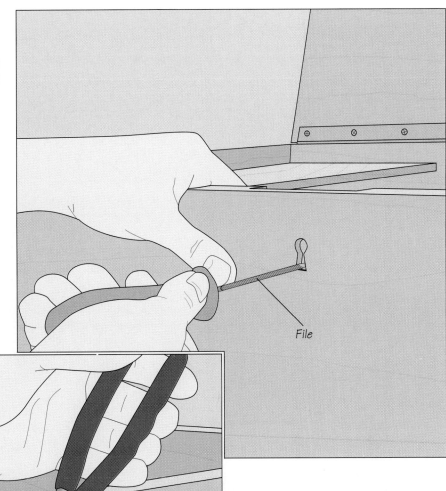

File

Escutcheon

4 Installing the escutcheon

Position the escutcheon on the front panel of the chest, aligning its opening over the keyhole. Use a strip of masking tape to hold the hardware in place while you start the nails in their holes. To protect your fingers when driving each nail flush, grip the nail shaft with needle-nose pliers *(left)*.

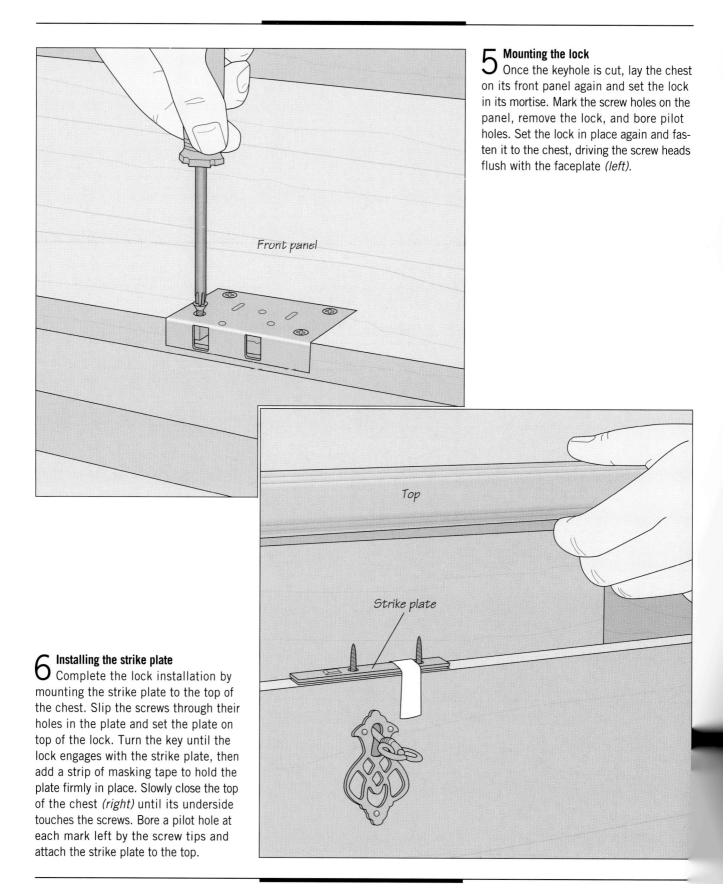

5 **Mounting the lock**
Once the keyhole is cut, lay the chest on its front panel again and set the lock in its mortise. Mark the screw holes on the panel, remove the lock, and bore pilot holes. Set the lock in place again and fasten it to the chest, driving the screw heads flush with the faceplate *(left)*.

Front panel

Top

Strike plate

6 **Installing the strike plate**
Complete the lock installation by mounting the strike plate to the top of the chest. Slip the screws through their holes in the plate and set the plate on top of the lock. Turn the key until the lock engages with the strike plate, then add a strip of masking tape to hold the plate firmly in place. Slowly close the top of the chest *(right)* until its underside touches the screws. Bore a pilot hole at each mark left by the screw tips and attach the strike plate to the top.

INSTALLING FLUSH HANDLES

1 Outlining the handles

Lay the chest on one side and position a handle outside-face-down midway between the front and back panels and a few inches below the top. Trace the outline of the mounting plate *(right)*.

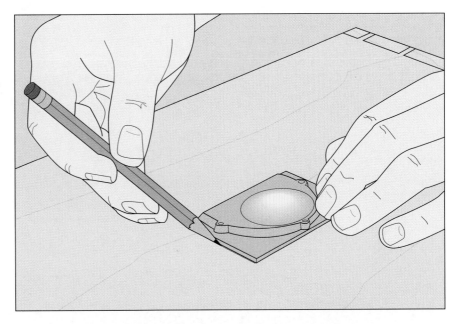

2 Mounting the handles

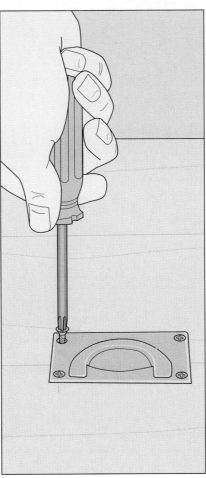

Install a straight bit in your router, set the cutting depth to the thickness of the mounting plate, and cut a mortise inside the marked outline as you would for a lock *(page 100)*. Next, measure the distance between the edges of the mounting plate and the bowl-shaped housing and transfer the measurement to the mortise. Adjust the router's cutting depth to the thickness of the housing and cut the deeper mortise. Test-fit the handle in the cavity and use a wood chisel to pare any remaining waste wood from the mortises *(far left)*. Once the mounting plate rests flush with the outside face of the side panel, mark the screw holes, remove the handle, and bore a pilot hole at each mark. Set the handle in place again and fasten it to the chest *(near left)*. Repeat the procedure for the other handle.

INLAYS

Commercial banding is available in a variety of designs to complement works ranging from a Welsh dresser to a boardroom table. Here, it adds a decorative touch to the top of a blanket chest. Inlay materials can be metal, wood veneer, or solid hardwood.

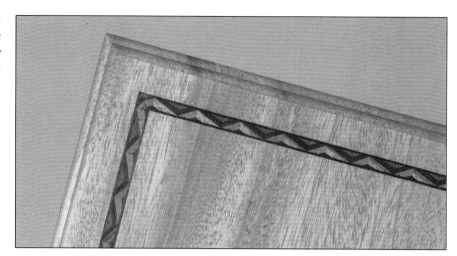

INSTALLING INLAY

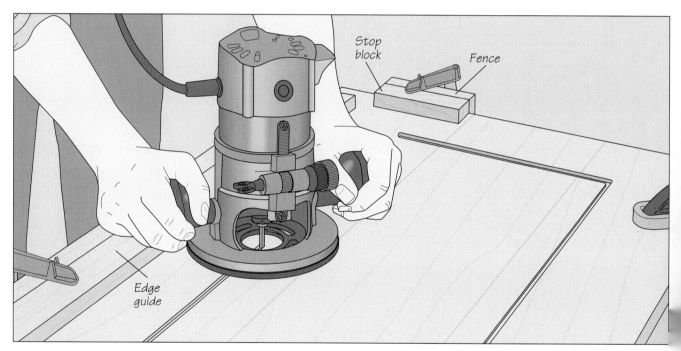

Stop block

Fence

Edge guide

1 Routing the groove

Grooves for inlay are cut with a router fitted with a straight bit the same width as the inlay. If you are installing shop-made inlay, set the cutting depth slightly shallower than the thickness of the strips; the inlay will be sanded flush *(step 3)*. For commercial banding, which is very thin, make the cutting depth equal to the inlay thickness to minimize sanding. Outline the groove on the top with a pencil; it should be equidistant from the edges. Rout the four sides of the groove individually, guiding the tool with an L-shaped edge guide and stop blocks. To set up the guides, align the bit with the cutting line, mea-

sure the distance between the router base plate and the edge of the top, and cut the edge guide and stop blocks to that width. Screw a fence to each piece so it can be positioned square to the edges of the top. For each cut, clamp the guide along the edge you will be cutting and fasten a stop block at each end. Holding the router's base plate against the edge guide and one stop block, turn on the tool and plunge the bit into the stock. Feed the bit *(above)* until the base plate contacts the other stop block. Once all the cuts are made, square the corners with a chisel.

2 Setting the inlay in the groove

Cut the inlay to length to fit in the groove, using your table saw for shop-made inlay, or a wood chisel for commercial banding. For the rectangular groove shown, make 45° miter cuts at the ends of the inlay pieces. Cut and test-fit one piece at a time, then spread a little glue on the underside of the inlay and insert it in the slot *(right)*, tapping the strip gently with a wooden mallet. Commercial banding should be held in place with masking tape until the adhesive cures.

3 Trimming the inlay

Once the glue has dried, sand the top to remove any excess adhesive and bring the inlay perfectly flush with the surface of the wood. For shop-made inlay, use a belt sander fitted with a 120-grit belt. Move the sander forward along one inlay piece *(left)* and pull the sander back when you reach the end of the strip, overlapping the first pass by one-half the width of the belt. Continue until the surfaces of the inlay and the top are flush, then move on to the other strips. Repeat the process with a finer belt (150- or 180-grit) to smooth the inlay and the surrounding surface. Sand commercial banding by hand with a sanding block. Be careful: Some modern banding is less than $\frac{1}{20}$ inch thick.

HIGHBOY

To prevent dust from entering the cabinet, special frames are installed underneath the bottom drawer in the lower chest. The dust shield is a basic frame-and-panel construction screwed to the carcase sides.

The highboy originated in 17th Century Europe and was inspired by the ornate Chinese lacquered cabinets imported for the English nobility. Because of its size, the highboy—or high chest of drawers—was constructed in two sections: a lower chest that supported a taller chest with four or more tiers. The top level was frequently divided into three smaller drawers set side by side.

As the Queen Anne style evolved into the more ornamental and classical Chippendale style during the latter part of the 18th Century, the highboy found favor with affluent society in colonial cities like Philadelphia, Boston, and New York. Towering 7 or 8 feet high, the imposing highboy was ideally suited to the elegant, lofty ceilings of the manor houses of the time, and its numerous drawers were the perfect solution for storing the articles needed for entertaining. Highboys became the hallmark of fashionable living rooms and their prices rose dramatically. The trend has continued unabated. Today, the highboys produced by the renowned Philadelphia cabinetmakers of the 1700s are among the most sought-after pieces of antique furniture.

The modern reproduction shown in the photograph on page 106 displays many traditional elements of the 18th Century design: the graceful cabriole legs, the scrolled pediment or crown molding, the flame-and-urn finials, the fluted quarter columns, and the shell carving and applied molding adorning the scalloped apron on the lower chest.

This chapter will show you how to design and construct this classic piece of furniture, from building the upper chest *(page 110)* to sawing and shaping the cabriole legs *(page 112)* and then assembling the lower chest *(page 116)*. Attention is also devoted to the finer details, like installing cockbeading around the drawers *(page 118)*, routing crown molding *(page 124)*, carving the finials *(page 130)*, and shaping the quarter columns *(page 134)*.

The following two pages illustrate the highboy's upper and lower chests. The major features of the piece are identified; refer to the pages indicated to find out how to make and install each element.

Building a highboy is a challenging task, but with care and diligence you can create a piece of furniture with the grace and timeless appeal of its 200-year-old ancestors.

The highboy at left exemplifies the harmony between straight lines and fluid curves typical of Queen Anne-style furniture.

ANATOMY OF A HIGHBOY

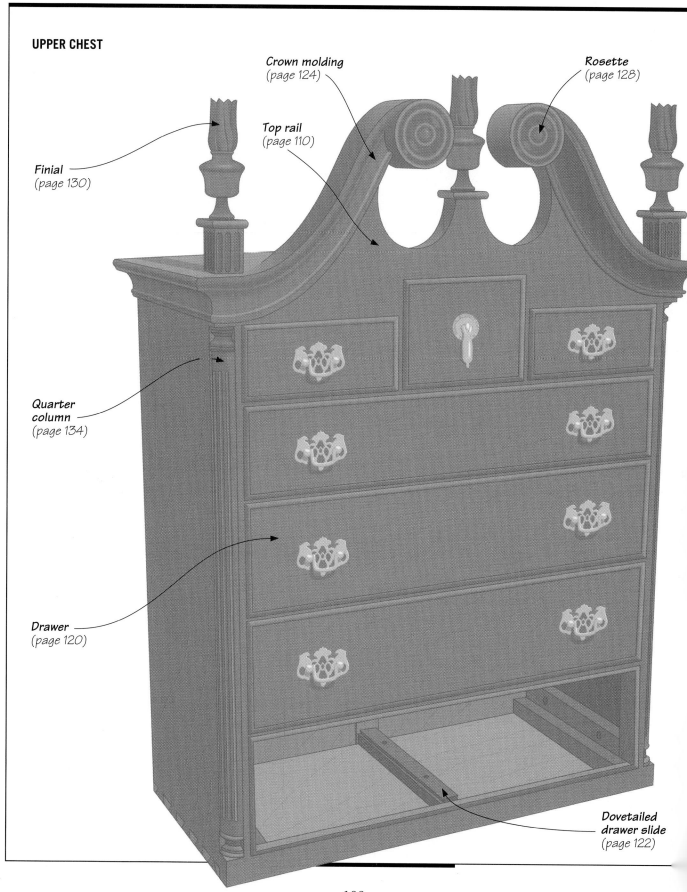

UPPER CHEST

Crown molding
(page 124)

Rosette
(page 128)

Top rail
(page 110)

Finial
(page 130)

Quarter column
(page 134)

Drawer
(page 120)

Dovetailed drawer slide
(page 122)

LOWER CHEST

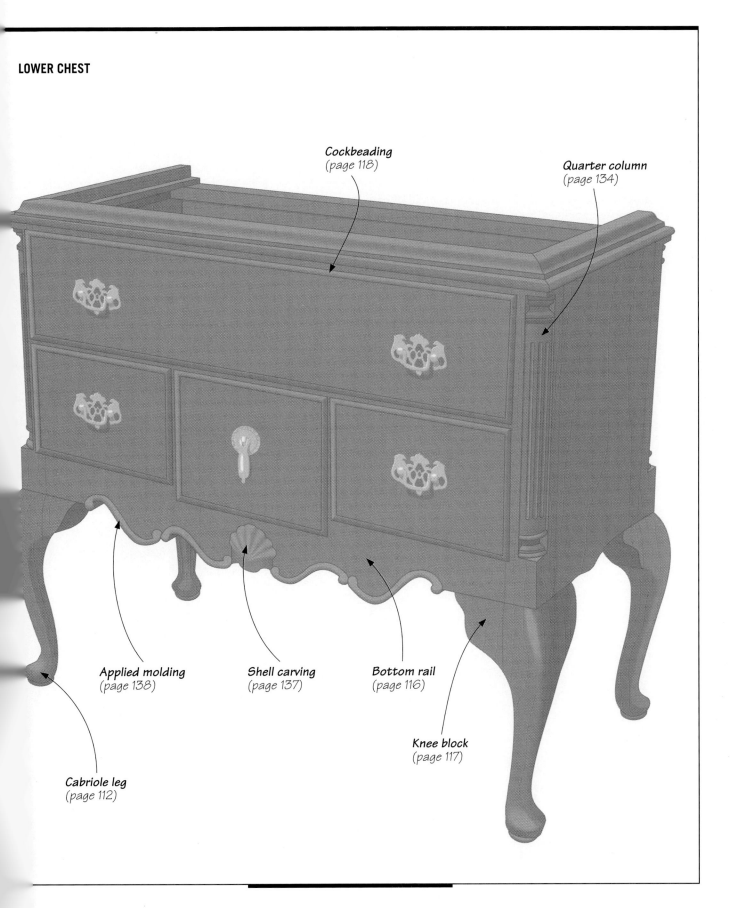

Cockbeading
(page 118)

Quarter column
(page 134)

Applied molding
(page 138)

Shell carving
(page 137)

Bottom rail
(page 116)

Knee block
(page 117)

Cabriole leg
(page 112)

ASSEMBLING THE UPPER CHEST

The highboy's upper chest has two major components: a large carcase and an elaborate face frame that fits within it. As shown below, the carcase consists of a top and bottom, two side panels, and two back panels separated by a stile—or muntin. The carcase corners are joined with through dovetail joints (*page 26*), and the back panels sit in rabbets cut around the inside edges of the carcase and muntin (*page 31*). The muntin is attached to the top and bottom of the carcase with mortise-and-tenon joints.

The face frame, shown face-up below and face-down on page 111, is built from a top rail, two L-shaped front posts, and a drawer frame for each tier of drawers. The top rail is shaped to accept the crown molding (*page 124*) and rosettes (*page 128*), both of which are added later. The back face of the top rail is grooved to accept the carcase top, and has a tenon cut in each end to fit in mortises in the two front posts. The L shape of the front posts creates the space for the quarter columns (*page 134*). The front posts sit in notches cut in the carcase top and bottom.

The drawer's supporting frames are assembled from rails and stiles joined with mortise-and-tenons (*page 36*). Each frame has an added dovetailed slide (*page 122*). To anchor the frames to the carcase, two braces are screwed to the top of each one and to the side panels. The drawer frames are notched at the front to accommodate the front posts and screwed to them. The uppermost drawer frame supports three small drawers; it features two dividers and three drawer slides. Once the face frame has been built, it is simply slipped into the carcase (*see below*) and then screwed to the side of the carcasc through the braces.

**CONSTRUCTION DETAIL
(FACE-UP VIEW)**

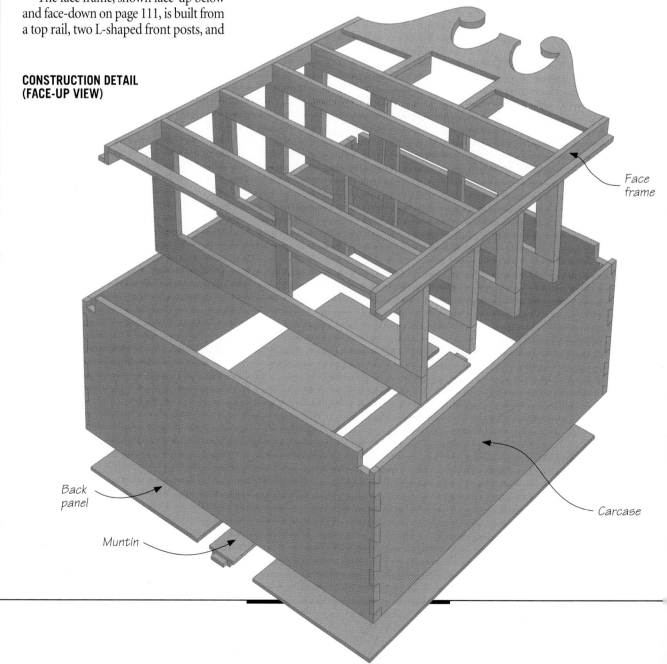

Face frame

Back panel

Muntin

Carcase

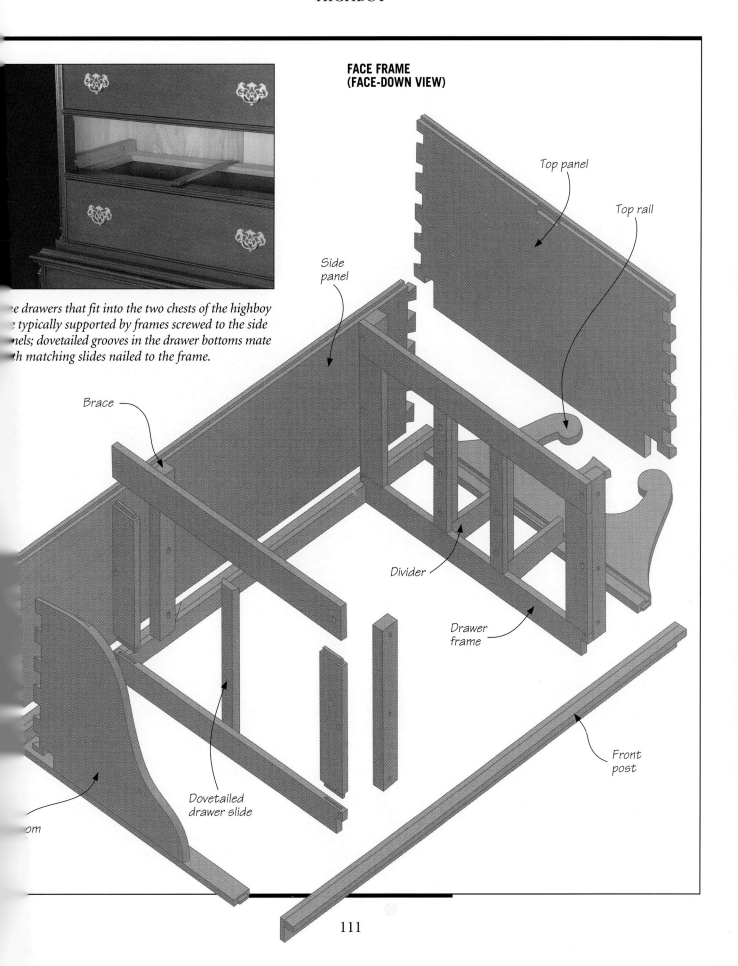

**FACE FRAME
(FACE-DOWN VIEW)**

Top panel

Top rail

Side panel

*...e drawers that fit into the two chests of the highboy
...e typically supported by frames screwed to the side
...nels; dovetailed grooves in the drawer bottoms mate
...th matching slides nailed to the frame.*

Brace

Divider

Drawer frame

Dovetailed drawer slide

Front post

...om

CABRIOLE LEGS

SAWING OUT THE LEGS

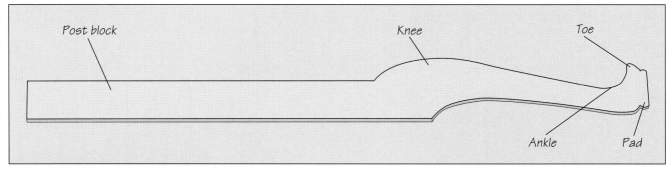

A diagram with labels: Post block, Knee, Toe, Ankle, Pad

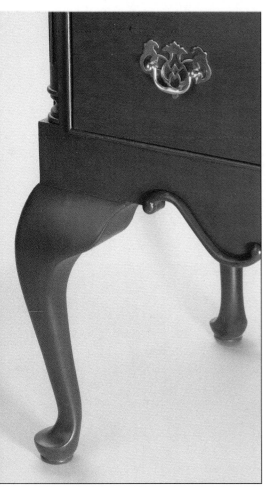

A distinctive feature of Queen Anne style, the tapering, curved cabriole leg has long been considered a challenge for cabinetmakers. But its graceful lines can be cut easily on the band saw and smoothed with hand tools.

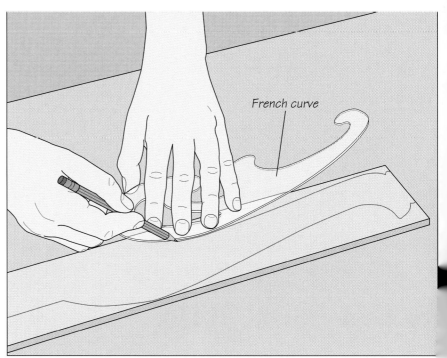

French curve

1 Designing the leg

Make a template from a piece of ¼-inch plywood or hardboard cut to the same length and width as your leg blanks. The design shown above at top will yield an attractive, stable, and well-proportioned leg, but you can alter the pattern to suit your project or copy the design of an existing leg that appeals to you. Begin drawing the leg by outlining the post block. Make its length equal to the width of the lower rail that will be attached to it, plus the height of the lower chest's side panels. The width of the post block should be adequate to accept the rail tenon. Later, it will be notched *(page 116)* to accept the quarter columns of the lower chest. Next, sketch the pad and the toe, then the front of the leg from the toe to the ankle using a french curve; at its narrowest point, the diameter of the ankle should be about two-fifths the stock width. Move on to the knee, sketching a gentle curve from the post block to the front edge of the template about 2 to 3 inches below the block. Then join the knee to the ankle with a relatively straight line. Complete the outline at the back of the leg, from the ankle to the bottom of the post block *(above)*. Experiment until you have a satisfactory design.

2 Transferring the design to the leg blanks

Cut out your template on a band saw, then sand the edges to the marked outline. Hold the template flat on one of the inside faces of the leg blank, making sure that the ends of the template and the blank are aligned and that the back of the post block is flush with the inside edge of the blank. Trace along the edges of the template to outline the leg. Turn the blank over and repeat the procedure on the other inside face *(right)*. At this point, some woodworkers prefer to prepare the legs and rails for the joinery before cutting the leg. (It is easier to clamp and cut a mortise in a rectangular leg blank, for example, than to carry out the same procedures on a leg with pronounced curves.) Other woodworkers cut the leg first and then do the joinery.

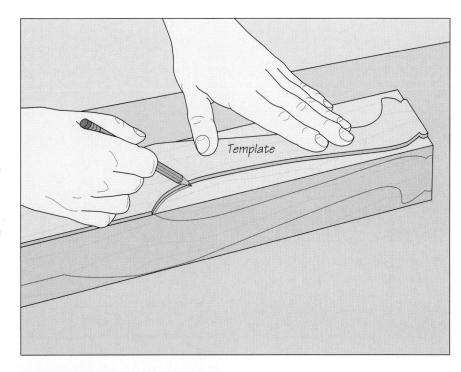

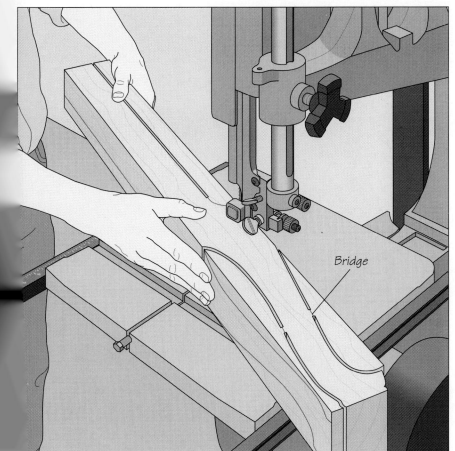

3 Cutting one face

Set the leg blank on the band saw table with one of the marked outlines facing up and the bottom of the leg pointing away from you. Aligning the saw blade just to the waste side of the marked line for the back of the leg, feed the stock into the blade. Turn off the saw about halfway through the cut and remove the workpiece. Then cut along the same line from the opposite end. To avoid detaching the waste piece from the blank and losing the marked outline on the adjacent face, stop the cut about ½ inch from the first kerf, leaving a short bridge between the two cuts. Retract the workpiece, then cut along the line for the front of the leg *(left)*, again leaving bridges to prevent the waste wood from falling away.

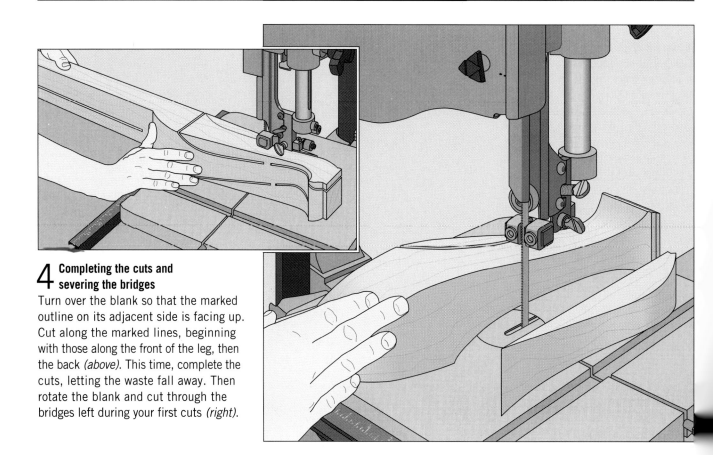

4 Completing the cuts and severing the bridges

Turn over the blank so that the marked outline on its adjacent side is facing up. Cut along the marked lines, beginning with those along the front of the leg, then the back *(above)*. This time, complete the cuts, letting the waste fall away. Then rotate the blank and cut through the bridges left during your first cuts *(right)*.

SHAPING THE LEGS

1 Forming the pad

Use a compass to outline the circular pad on the bottom of the leg. Then secure the leg in a vise, with the bottom end facing up, and use a backsaw to cut away the bulk of the waste surrounding the outline. Make two series of cuts, starting with four cuts straight into the end of the leg at the corners, then sawing around the end of the leg to sever the corners. Next, secure the leg in a bar clamp, lock the clamp in a vise, and use a patternmaker's rasp to round the corners of the pad. Continue until the pad is circular *(right)*, rotating the leg in the clamp as necessary. Use a file to smooth the pad.

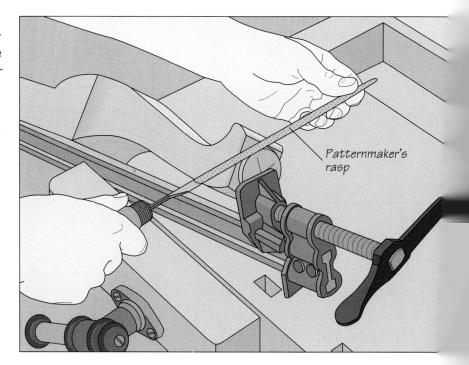

Patternmaker's rasp

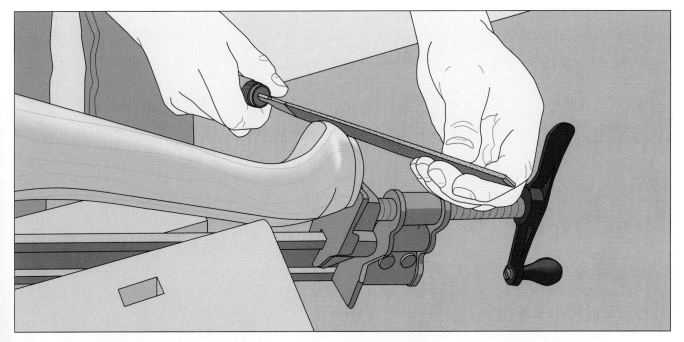

2 Shaping the foot

Reposition the clamp in the vise so the foot is tilted down. Holding the patternmaker's rasp at an angle of approximately 45° to the leg, begin by shaping the contour from the bottom up *(above)*. Rotate the leg in the clamp as necessary so that you can shape the foot all the way around. Smooth the surface using a double-cut flat bastard file, then finish the job with sandpaper, using progressively finer-grit papers.

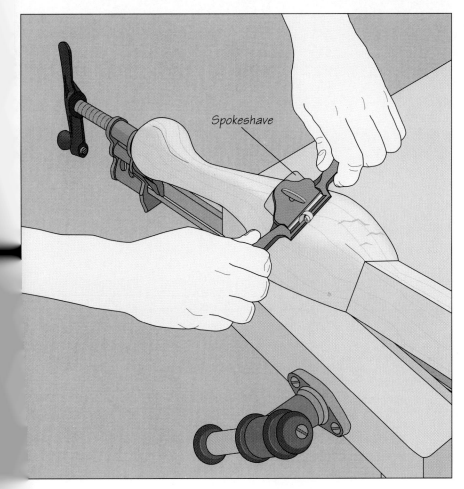

Spokeshave

3 Shaping and smoothing the knee

To finish shaping the cabriole leg and to remove any blemishes left by the band saw blade, smooth the surface of the knee with a spokeshave, following with a rasp and sandpaper. Holding the spokeshave with both hands at the bottom of a curved edge of the leg, push the tool slowly away from you, cutting a thin shaving *(left)*. Make a series of overlapping passes, working with the grain until the surface is smooth. Turn the leg in the bar clamp to clean up the other edges. Use the rasp to smooth an area that the spokeshave cannot reach. Complete the job with sandpaper.

ASSEMBLING THE LOWER CHEST

Once the cabriole legs are completed and the cavities for the quarter columns are routed in the post blocks, the lower chest can be glued up. The chest —shown in the photo on page 107—is made up of four legs, two side panels, two back panels, bottom rails at the front and back, and two drawer frames. The bottom drawer frame contains dust panels and is divided into sections for three drawers. Like the drawer frames of the upper chest, the top frame features a dovetailed drawer slide. (The three small lower drawers slide well without the aid of a slide.) The frames are screwed to braces that are attached to the side panels. The legs are grooved to accept the entire thickness of the back panels and rabbets in the side panels. The legs also feature mortises that mate with tenons cut in the bottom rails. As with the upper chest, the back panels are separated by a muntin. Once the lower chest is glued up, knee blocks are fashioned and attached to the legs (*page 117*). Cockbeading around the drawers and the shell carving and applied molding on the bottom rail are added later. To complete the chest, the quarter columns are turned and installed in the leg notches and, finally, a molded frame is attached to the top edge of the chest. The frame will conceal the seam when the upper chest is set in place.

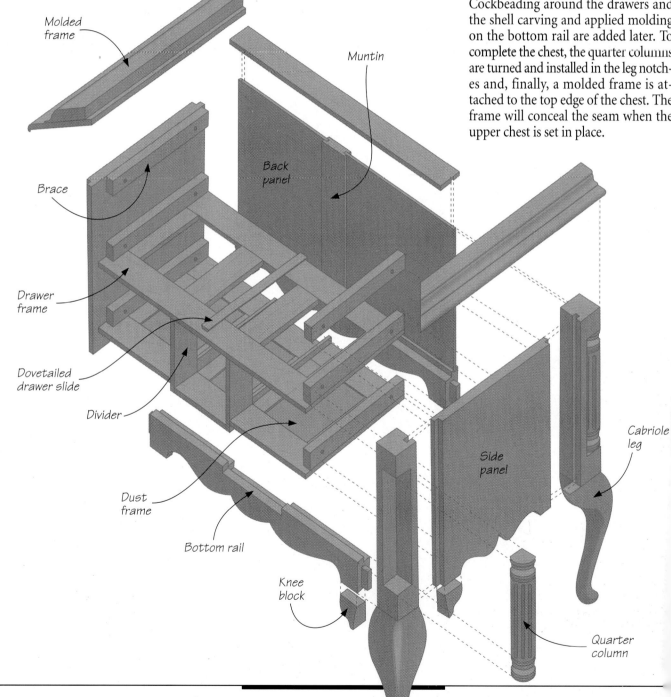

116

MAKING AND MOUNTING KNEE BLOCKS

Designing the knee blocks

The knee blocks, which join the curves of the legs and bottom rails, are designed and cut much like the legs themselves. For a template, place a piece of stiff cardboard in the corner between the leg and adjoining rail and draw a contour line that connects the two pieces. The same template can be used for all the knee blocks. Transfer the line to a wood blank that is as thick as the leg, slightly wider and larger than the area it must fill. Place the blank against the rail and leg so its outside face is flush with the outer part of the leg and draw a second line on the blank using the leg as a guide *(right)*. The grain of the block should be parallel to that of the leg. Saw out the block on the band saw as you did the legs *(page 113)*.

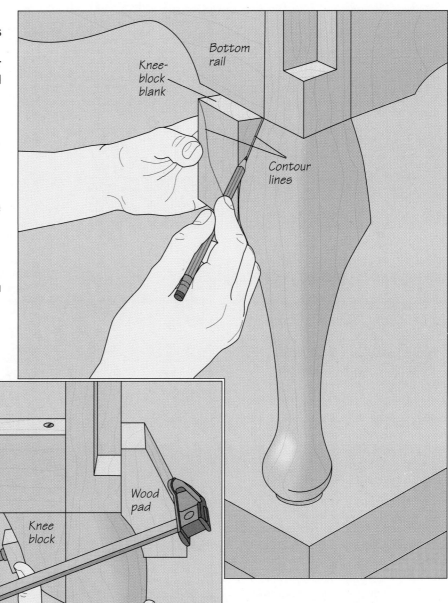

2 Mounting the knee blocks

Once all the knee blocks have been cut and smoothed, glue them up one at a time. Apply a thin layer of adhesive to the contacting surfaces, then hold the pieces in place with a clamp. Use wood pads to protect the stock and direct clamping pressure by shaping them to fit flush against the legs *(left)*. Drive a screw through the knee block and into the leg for added reinforcement.

COCKBEADING

Cockbeading is a rounded molding that extends beyond the front of the highboy and frames the drawer openings. It is set into rabbets cut along the inside edges of the openings. In addition to providing decoration, cockbeading protects the edges of veneered drawer fronts.

Acrylic sub-base

MAKING AND INSTALLING COCKBEADING

1 Preparing the drawer openings
Use a router fitted with a ¼-inch piloted rabbeting bit to cut the rabbets around the drawer openings. Set the depth of cut at ½ inch, then attach a square piece of ¼-inch clear acrylic to the tool's base plate *(inset)*. Make this auxiliary sub-base large enough to keep the tool flat and stable during the operation. Set the chest on its back on a work surface. Starting at the corner of one drawer opening, rest the router on the chest with the bit just clear of the workpiece. Grip the tool firmly with both hands and turn it on, guiding the bit into the wood. Once the pilot bearing butts against the stock, feed the router toward the adjacent corner, keeping the sub-base flat *(right)*. Continue around the opening until you reach your starting point. Cut rabbets around the other drawer openings the same way, then square the corners with a chisel.

2 Making the cockbeading

Make enough cockbeading from ¼-inch-thick stock to fit in all the rabbets cut in step 1. The cockbeading is best shaped using molding cutters on the table saw. (Do not use narrow stock; instead, cut pieces that are at least 4 inches wide and then rip the cockbeading from them.) Install an auxiliary wood fence and fit the molding head with cutters on your table saw. Raise the head into the wood fence to notch it. Use a featherboard to secure the workpiece; screw it to a shim so that pressure will be applied against the middle of the workpiece. Make a few test passes with scrap stock to set the width of cut. For the first pass, center the board edge over a cutter, then butt the fence against the face of the stock. Hold the board flush against the fence and the table as you feed it into the cutters *(right)*. Experiment with different cutting widths until the edge of the stock is properly rounded, then shape both edges of each workpiece. Once all your stock has been milled, install a rip blade on the saw and cut the cockbeading from the boards, making it wide enough to protrude by ¼ inch from the drawer openings when glued into the rabbets.

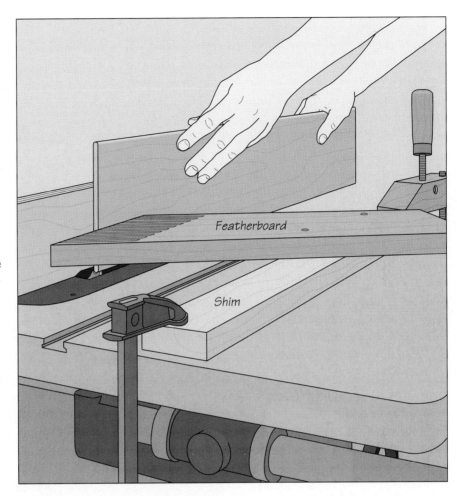

Featherboard

Shim

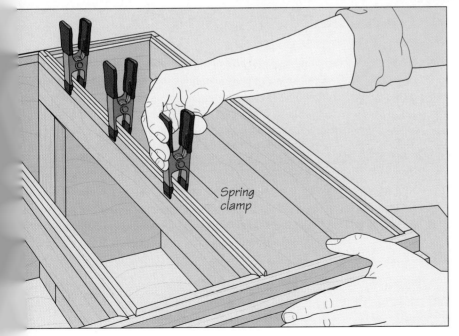

Spring clamp

3 Mounting the cockbeading

Cut the cockbeading to length, mitering the ends with the table saw or a backsaw and miter box. It is easiest to cut and fit one piece at a time, making sure you align the mitered ends with the corners of the rabbets. Spread a little glue on the contacting surfaces and insert one strip at a time, securing the pieces in place with spring clamps at 6-inch intervals *(left)*.

MAKING THE DRAWERS

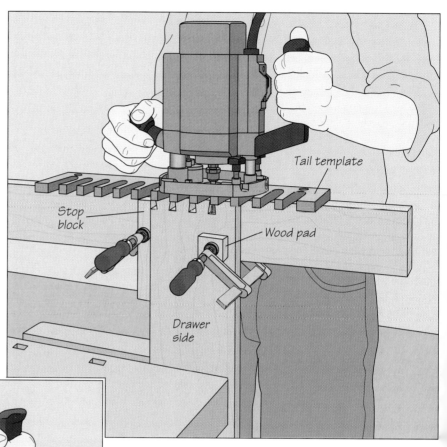

The highboy's drawers exemplify classic cabinetmaking techniques. The corners are joined with through dovetails and the end grain of the tail boards is then hidden with a false front. A dovetailed runner attached to the bottom glides along a mating slide fastened to the frame.

Tail template

Stop block

Wood pad

Drawer side

Pin template

Drawer front or back

1 Cutting the dovetail joints

Size the drawer parts to fit the openings in the chests, then rout the dovetails, cutting the pins in the front and back pieces and the tails in the sides. A set of commercial templates like the one shown on this page makes the job simple and ensures accurate results. Attach the pin and tail templates to backup boards following the manufacturer's instructions. Secure one of the drawer sides end-up in a vise. Clamp the backup board to the stock, making sure there are half-tails at either end; the template and backup board should be flush against the work-piece. Protecting the stock with a wood pad, butt a stop block against the drawer side and clamp it to the support board to help you align subsequent cuts. Install the dovetail bit and template guide supplied with the jig and cut the tails, feeding the tool in and out of the template slots *(above)*. Cut the remaining tails the same way. Then use one of the completed tail boards to outline the pins on one drawer front or back. Secure the pin board in the vise and clamp the pin template to the stock, aligning the jig fingers with the marked outline. Install the straight bit supplied with the jig and rout out the waste between the pins *(left)*. Repeat at the other end and for the remaining fronts and backs.

2 Preparing the drawers for bottom panels

Dry-fit the parts of each drawer and clamp the unit, aligning the bars of the clamps with the front and back pieces; remember to protect the stock with wood pads. Then rout a groove for the bottom panel along the inside of the drawer. Fit a router with a three-wing slotting cutter and mount the tool in a table. Adjust the cutting height to leave the thickness of the drawer runners you will make in step 3 below the groove. Set the drawer right-side up on the table and, starting at the middle of one drawer side, feed the stock into the cutter. Keeping the pilot bearing butted against the workpiece, feed the drawer clockwise *(right)*. Continue pivoting the drawer on the table until you return to your starting point.

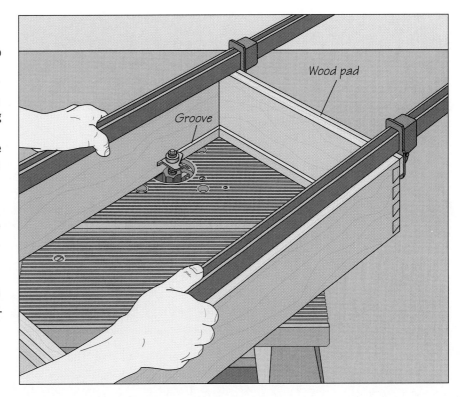

Wood pad

Groove

3 Making the drawer runners and slides

Mounting the drawers in the highboy requires two additional components for each drawer: a runner with a dovetailed groove on the drawer bottom and a matching slide for the frame. Prepare the runner first; it should be as long as the drawer sides and the same thickness as the gap between the bottom panel and the bottom edge of the drawer. To cut the groove in the runner, install a dovetail bit in a router and mount the tool in a table. Set the cutting depth at one-half the runner's thickness. Adjust the fence to center the groove in the runner and make two passes to rout it, using a push block to feed the stock *(left)*. Make the matching slide on the table saw, using stock one-half as thick as the runner. Adjust the blade to the same angle as the sides of the groove, then make two passes to cut the slide, positioning the rip fence on the left-hand side of the blade so the cutting edge is angled away from the fence. Feed the stock using a push stick *(inset)*.

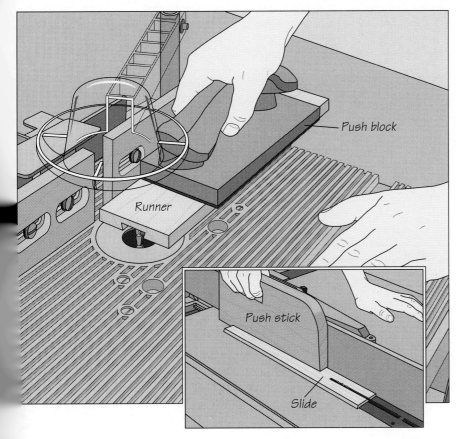

Push block

Runner

Push stick

Slide

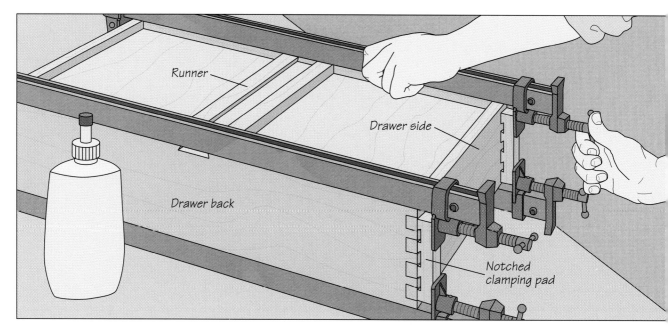

4 Gluing up the drawers

For the bottom panel of each drawer, cut a piece of ¼-inch plywood to fit the opening, adding the depth of the grooves to its length and width. Dry-fit and clamp the drawer again, position the runner across the bottom panel, and mark the sides of the runner's dovetailed groove on the drawer back. Disassemble the drawer and use a chisel to extend the dovetailed groove through the drawer back. If you wish to install drawer stops *(page 123)*, prepare them now. Then glue up the drawer as you did the chests, adding some adhesive to attach the runners to the drawer bottoms. Notched clamping pads will ensure that pressure is only applied to the tail boards *(above)*.

5 Installing the drawer slides

Once the adhesive has dried, slip each drawer slide into its runner on the drawer bottom and install the drawer in the highboy. Mark the location of the slide on the front and back of the drawer frame, then remove the drawer. Remove the slide and center it on the frame between the alignment marks. Apply a thin layer of glue on the contacting surfaces and secure the slide in place with clamps *(right)*. Once the clamps have been tightened, screw the slide to the front and back of the frame.

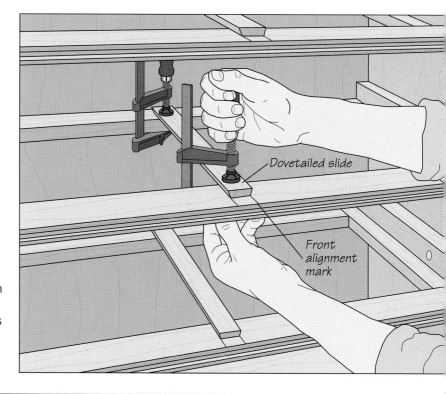

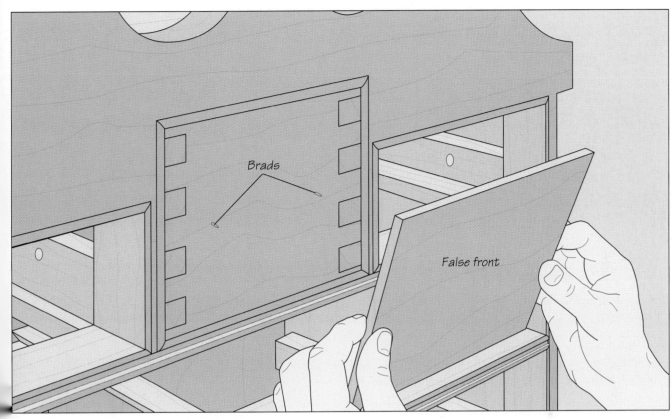

Brads

False front

6 Installing the false fronts
Attach a false front to each drawer to conceal the end grain of the drawer sides. Set the drawer face up on a work surface and drive two brads into the drawer front, leaving their heads protruding. Make sure the brads are not located where the drawer pull will be installed, then snip off the heads and reinstall the drawer. Cut the false front to the right size, then carefully position it over the drawer front *(above)*. Once you are satisfied with the placement, press firmly; the pointed ends of the brads will punch impressions into the back of the false front. Remove the drawer and glue the false front in place, aligning the impressions with the brads.

SHOP TIP

Adjustable drawer stop
To keep a drawer from being pulled right out, attach a simple stop to the frame. Before gluing up the drawer, cut a 1-inch-square notch in the middle of the top edge of the drawer back. Saw the stop from scrap, making it longer and narrower than 1 inch. Mount the stop to the bottom of the frame or panel under which the drawer will slide. Line it up with the notch in the drawer back. Screw the stop in place, leaving the fastener loose enough so the stop can be rotated. When you install the drawer, turn the stop so that the long edge is parallel to the drawer sides. Once the stop passes through the notch, turn it 90° so its long edge is parallel to the back.

The crown molding—or pediment—on each side of the highboy front is actually built up from four separate pieces of wood. The broken swan-neck face molding that curves upwards from the front corner to the rosette is made from two pieces of molding glued together. With the help of a template cut on the band saw, the molding pieces are shaped on a pin router (page 125). The moldings on both sides of the highboy, called the returns, also consist of two pieces glued together. They are installed with dovetailed slides that fit into matching grooves in the upper chest (page 127).

A COLLECTION OF CROWN MOLDING STYLES

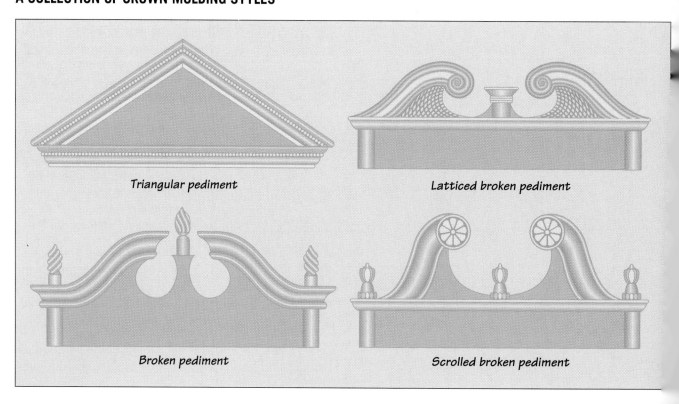

Triangular pediment

Latticed broken pediment

Broken pediment

Scrolled broken pediment

FACE MOLDINGS

1 Shaping the first piece of molding

For a template, trace the contours of the upper rail onto a piece of ¾-inch plywood. Add a cutting line to represent the bottom edge of the first piece of molding *(inset)*, then saw the template in two along the line and discard the bottom half. Outline the template on the stock you will use for the molding and cut it to size. Next, screw the molding blank atop the template, making sure the fasteners will be clear of the router bit. Install a piloted panel-raising bit and mount the router in a pin routing attachment. Follow the manufacturer's directions for setting the depth of cut, then place the starter pin in the table on the infeed side of the bit. As you feed the molding blank into the bit, brace the template against the pin *(right)*, keeping the molding blank against the bit's pilot bearing. Make light cuts, using as many passes as necessary to reach your final depth. Repeat the process with the template reversed to shape the molding for the other side of the chest front. Then shape the side moldings using the same setup and a straight template of the same thickness.

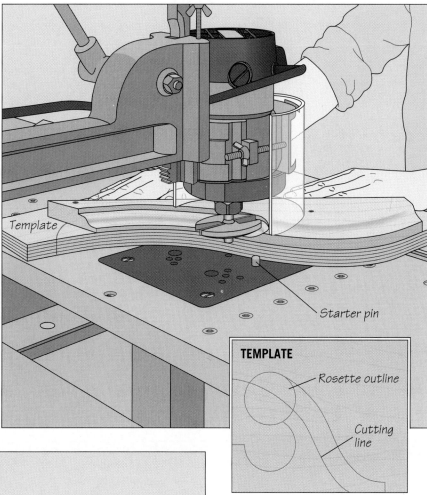

Template

Starter pin

TEMPLATE

Rosette outline

Cutting line

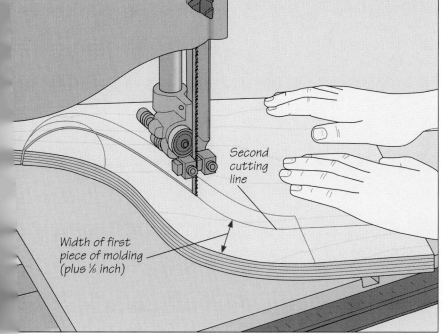

Second cutting line

Width of first piece of molding (plus ⅛ inch)

2 Shaping the second piece of molding

The piece of molding that is glued to the first one to build up the face molding is shaped by the same process used in step 1. Unscrew the first piece from the template, then draw a cutting line for the second piece, offsetting the line by the width of the first piece plus ⅛ inch. Band saw along the mark *(left)*. Cut and shape the second piece of molding as you did the first: Cut it to width, attach the piece to the template, and shape it on the pin routing attachment—this time, using a round-over bit. Once the molding has been shaped, unscrew it from the template and saw it to final width.

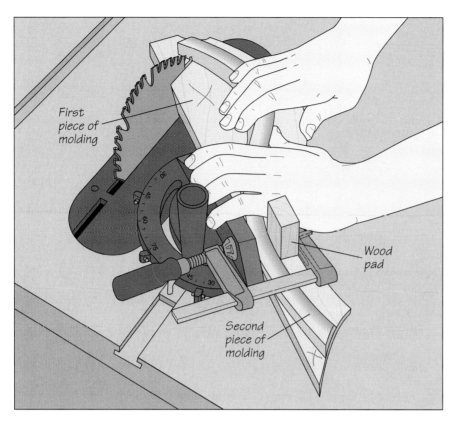

First piece of molding

Wood pad

Second piece of molding

3 Preparing the face moldings for installation

Glue the parts of the face molding together and hold them securely with clamps. Once the adhesive has cured, each piece of face molding must be cut at one end to meet the side molding and at the other end to fit around the rosette. For the side molding-end, set up your table saw for a compound cut by angling the blade to 45° and the miter gauge to the angle formed between the straight edge of the molding and the side of the carcase when the molding is held in place. Clamp the face molding to the miter gauge, protecting the stock with a wood pad. Since the top of the molding is straight and the bottom is curved, you will have to feed the stock with what would normally be the trailing end first. Hold the gauge and molding securely, and push the stock into the cut, keeping your hands well clear of the blade *(left)*. Then band saw the waste (marked with Xs).

INSTALLING THE CROWN MOLDING

1 Installing the face molding

Once all the moldings have been shaped and cut to length, install the quarter columns *(page 134)*. Then clamp the side molding in place using protective wood pads. Next, mount the face molding to the rail as you did the false fronts of the drawers *(page 123)*, using brads to align the stock *(right)*. The mitered end of the face molding should rest flush against the end of the side molding. Glue and clamp the face molding to the rail.

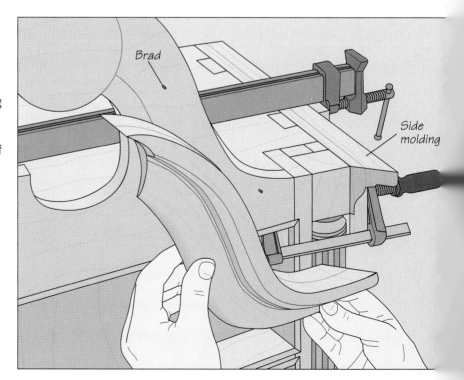

Brad

Side molding

2 Preparing the upper chest for the side molding

The side molding is attached to the chest with a sliding dovetail joint to allow the carcase to expand and contract because of changes in humidity without breaking the mitered joints on the front corners. The dovetailed groove is cut in the chest side with a router. Install a dovetail bit, then attach a commercial edge guide to the tool's base plate and screw a wood extension to the guide fence to increase its bearing surface. Set the chest on its side and place the router on top. Adjust the edge guide so that the groove will be cut just below the corner joint. With the bit clear of the chest, start at the back and feed the cutting edges into the side panel, pulling the edge guide extension flush against the top panel. Continue toward the front of the chest *(right)*, stopping the cut a little past the halfway point.

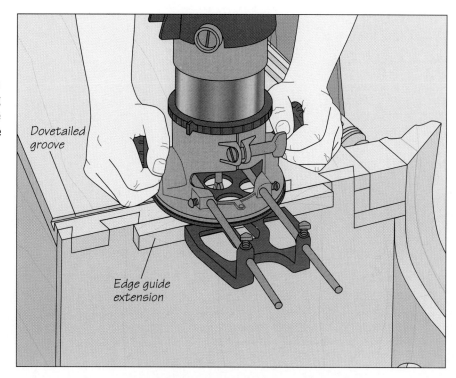

Dovetailed groove

Edge guide extension

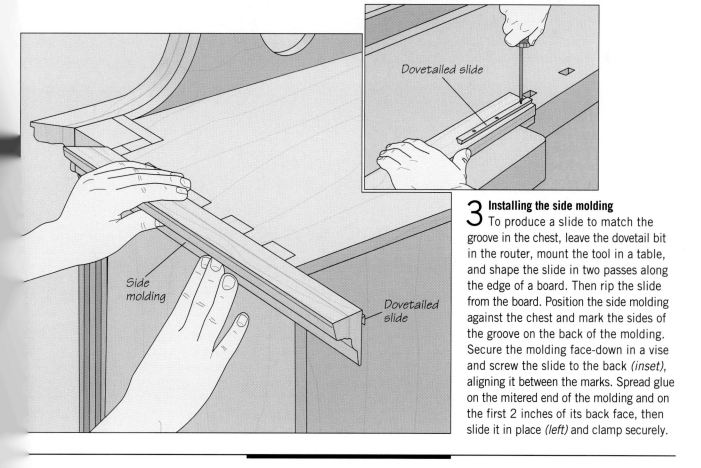

Dovetailed slide

Side molding

Dovetailed slide

3 Installing the side molding

To produce a slide to match the groove in the chest, leave the dovetail bit in the router, mount the tool in a table, and shape the slide in two passes along the edge of a board. Then rip the slide from the board. Position the side molding against the chest and mark the sides of the groove on the back of the molding. Secure the molding face-down in a vise and screw the slide to the back *(inset)*, aligning it between the marks. Spread glue on the mitered end of the molding and on the first 2 inches of its back face, then slide it in place *(left)* and clamp securely.

ROSETTES

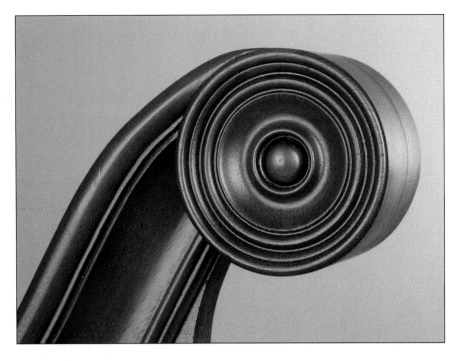

Rosettes are an ornamental feature common to many furniture styles. They can take many shapes and be produced in various ways. The concentric circles of the rosette at left were turned on a lathe, creating a pattern that flows seamlessly from the graceful curves of the crown molding.

MAKING THE ROSETTES

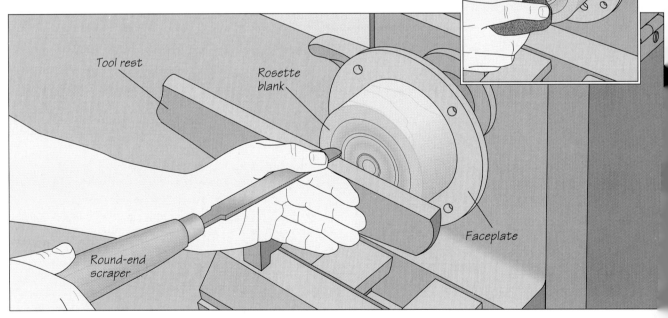

Tool rest

Rosette blank

Faceplate

Round-end scraper

Turning the rosettes

Cut the rosette blanks to fit on the end of the face moldings. Attach a blank to the center of a lathe faceplate, then mount the plate on the machine. Adjust the tool rest so the top face of the scraper you will use is level with the center of the blank. The rest should be as close to the wood as possible without touching it. Switch on the lathe. Holding the tip of a round-end scraper against the blank, round over the rosette's outside edge, and then cut the concentric rings on its face *(above)*. Hold the scraper blade on the tool rest to keep it steady. Cut on the left-hand side of the blank to prevent the scraper from kicking up. Once the rings have been carved, remove the tool rest and smooth the face of the blank with fine-grit sandpaper *(inset)*.

MOUNTING THE ROSETTES

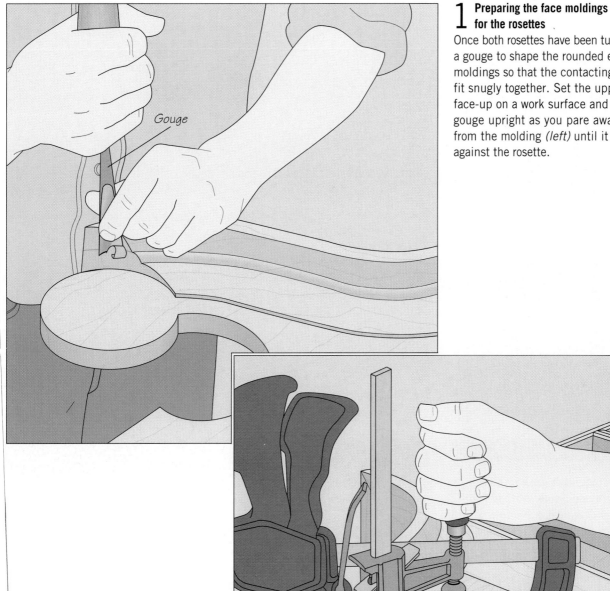

1 Preparing the face moldings for the rosettes
Once both rosettes have been turned, use a gouge to shape the rounded end of the moldings so that the contacting surfaces fit snugly together. Set the upper chest face-up on a work surface and hold the gouge upright as you pare away wood from the molding *(left)* until it fits flush against the rosette.

Gouge

Wood pad

2 Gluing up the rosettes
Position each rosette in turn on the chest so that its wood grain runs in the same direction as the face molding. This will create the impression that the two parts are one continuous piece. Mark the rosette where it touches the molding, then apply some glue to the contacting surfaces of both pieces. Use one clamp to secure the rosette in place and a second *(right)* to keep it from sliding forward or backward. Protect the stock with wood pads.

SHAPING THE POMMEL

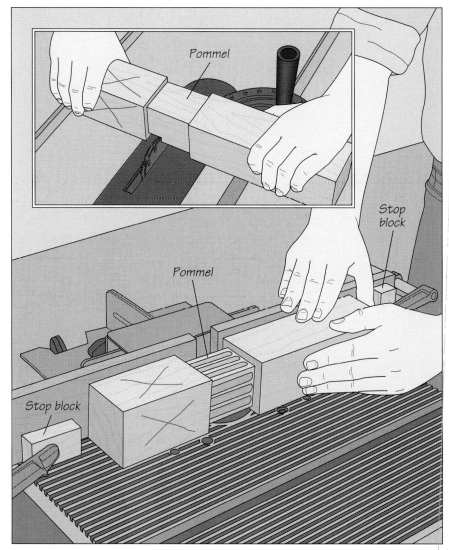

Traditionally used to decorate the corners of furniture, finials take a variety of forms, including flame-and-urn, acorn, pineapple, and plume. The finial above incorporates two shapes, a flame-and-urn on a fluted pommel base. This example is produced from the bottom up: First, the flutes of the pommel are grooved on a router table (right), and then the flame and urn are turned on a lathe (page 131). Finally, the finished shape of the flame is carved by hand (page 133).

Cutting the flutes

Make a blank for each finial that is slightly larger than the finished dimensions. Mark the top and bottom of the pommel on the blank and use Xs to indicate the waste section below the pommel. Use the dado head in a table saw to reduce the blank's thickness between the two marks. Set the cutting depth at ⅜ inch. Feed the blank with the miter gauge, cutting away the waste with overlapping passes on each face *(inset)*. The flutes are cut with a core box bit in a table-mounted router. Set the cutting depth at ¼ inch. Align the pommel over the bit for the first set of outside flutes and lock the fence against the blank. To ensure that all the flutes will be the same length, clamp a stop block to the fence at each end of the blank. Turn on the router and lower the blank onto the bit with its trailing end against the stop block closest to you and its edge against the fence. Feed the blank until it contacts the other stop block. Lift the blank, then rotate it and repeat the process until one set of outside flutes is finished. Reposition the fence once to rout the middle flutes and again for the second set of outside flutes *(above)*.

TURNING THE FLAME-AND-URN

1 Turning the cylinder

Cut off most of the waste section be-low the pommel, leaving a couple of inches for a round tenon. Mount the blank on a lathe and adjust the tool rest as close to the workpiece as possible without touching it. Use a roughing-out gouge to round the corners of the blank above the pommel. Turn on the lathe and hold the tip of the gouge against the rotating blank. Begin with the tip of the gouge tilted up, then gradually raise the handle until the bev-el under the tip is rubbing against the stock and the cutting edge is slicing into it. Work from the right-hand end of the blank toward the pommel, leaving a square shoulder above the pommel *(right)*. Keep the tool at the same angle to the work-piece throughout the cut. Continue until the blank is cylindrical and smooth.

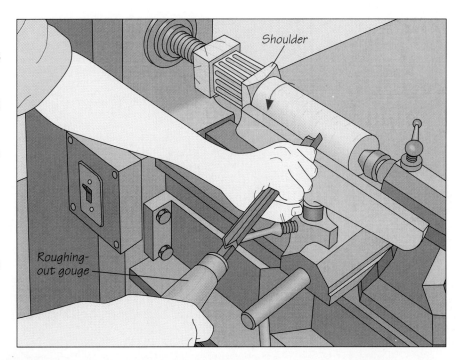

2 Shaping the flame

Leave the blank rotating while you mark the bottom ends of the urn and the flame with a pencil. Use a skew chisel to cut a notch separating the flame and urn, then begin shaping the flame with a spindle gouge *(above)*. The process is the same as for the cylinder in step 1, but instead of holding the tool at a fixed angle to the blank, sweep it from side to side while angling the tip to cut a contour. Continue until the flame has the desired shape.

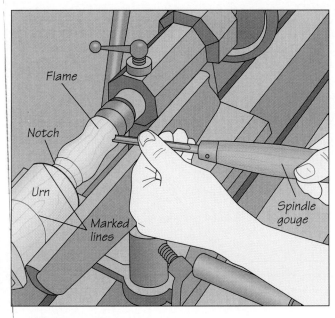

3 Shaping the urn

Shape the urn with a spindle gouge as you did the flame. Then use a skew chisel to cut a notch defining the lower end of the urn. Pressing the chisel firmly against the tool rest, hold the short point of the tip against the blank to cut the V-shaped notch; keep the bevel on the back of the blade rubbing against the stock to help control the cut *(above)*. Then use the skew chisel and spindle gouge to shape beads below the urn.

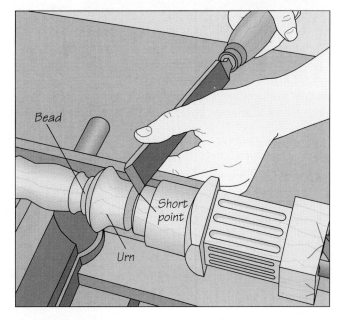

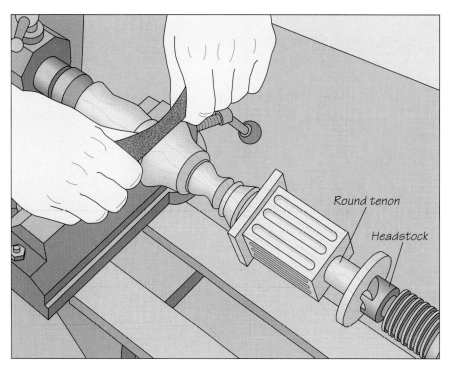

4 Turning the tenon and smoothing the finial

Use a parting tool to turn a ¾-inch-long round tenon below the pommel, leaving a thin disk of wood against the headstock of the lathe. Then remove the tool rest and smooth the surface of the finial with sandpaper, using progressively finer grits. Fold the paper to reach around the beads and into crevices *(left)*. To finish smoothing the piece, hold a handful of wood shavings under the rotating finial and allow it to rub against the shavings. Combined with your skin oils, the shavings will impart a smooth finish to the surface. Once the job is done, turn off and unplug the lathe, but leave the blank mounted on the tool.

CARVING THE FLAME

1 Sketching the pattern

To help you carve the flame, mark a grid of ½-inch squares on the entire surface of the flame section. Then draw in four equally spaced spiral lines from the bottom to the top of the section to delineate the hollows you will carve in step 2; the lines should intersect opposite corners of each square *(right)*.

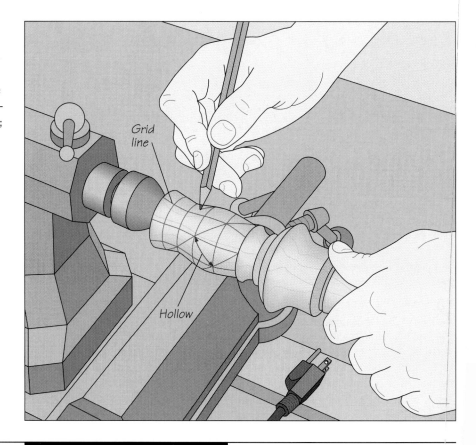

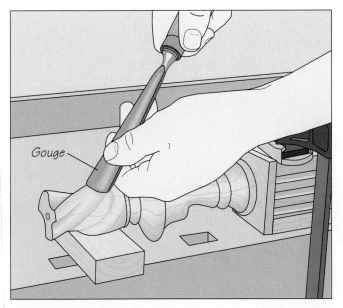 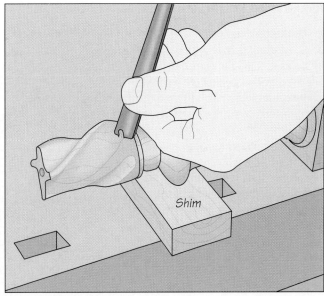

2 Carving the flame

Remove the finial from the lathe and saw off the waste disk below the tenon. Then clamp the finial to a work surface, using shims to hold it parallel to the benchtop. Carve the hollows between the grid lines with two gouges, starting with a wide-blade tool *(above, left)*. Work parallel to the wood grain as much as possible; rotate and re-clamp the finial so that you can reach the entire surface. Use a narrower gouge to carve a sharply defined ridge between each hollow *(above, right)*. Work from the bottom to the top of the flame, bringing each ridge to a point. Then hollow out the top end to remove the hole left by the lathe's tailstock and smooth the flame with sandpaper.

MOUNTING THE FINIALS

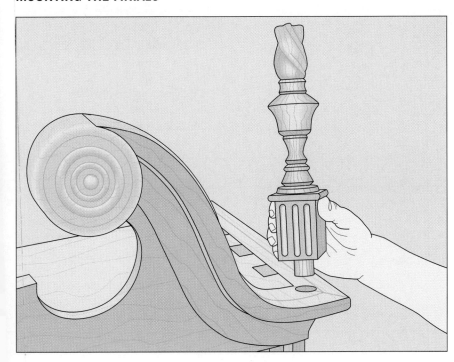

Gluing the finials to the chest

For each finial, bore a hole into the top of the chest with a spade bit the same diameter as the tenon on the finial. Locate the hole directly above the quarter column *(page 134)*. This will create the impression that the column and finial are a single piece. Spread glue on the tenon and the sides of the hole, then fit the finial in place *(left)*. Use a clamp to hold it in position until the adhesive cures.

QUARTER COLUMNS

MAKING AND INSTALLING THE QUARTER COLUMNS

1 Making the columns

Cut a blank several inches longer than the finished length of the columns, and wide and thick enough for the number of quarter columns you need. Rip the blank into quarters, joint the inside surfaces of the pieces, then glue and clamp them back together with newspaper in between *(inset, top)*. This will enable you to pull the columns apart easily. Once the glue is dry, mount the blank on a lathe. Mark two lines on the blank for the length of the column and indicate the waste with Xs *(inset, bottom)*. Drive screws through the waste sections to hold the quarters together. Adjust a set of outside calipers to the desired diameter of the column, then turn the blank into a cylinder as you did for the finials *(page 131)*. Periodically turn off the lathe and use the calipers to check the diameter of the blank *(right)*. Once you have reduced the blank to the correct diameter, turn two beads at each end using a skew chisel and a fingernail gouge. Then cut the flutes in the blank, either by hand using a gouge or with the router and jig shown on page 135.

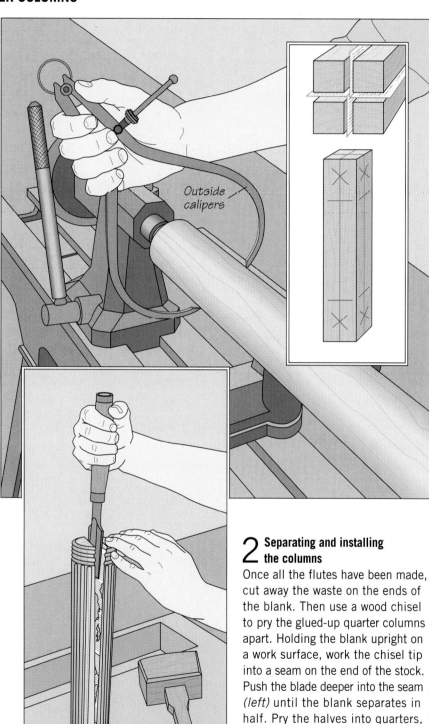

Outside calipers

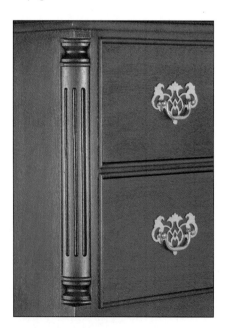

Fluted quarter columns add a strong visual framework to the highboy.

2 Separating and installing the columns

Once all the flutes have been made, cut away the waste on the ends of the blank. Then use a wood chisel to pry the glued-up quarter columns apart. Holding the blank upright on a work surface, work the chisel tip into a seam on the end of the stock. Push the blade deeper into the seam *(left)* until the blank separates in half. Pry the halves into quarters, then use a scraper to clean the glue and newspaper from the columns. To install the columns on the chest, spread some glue on their inside surfaces and clamp them in place.

BUILD IT YOURSELF

A ROUTER-LATHE JIG FOR FLUTING QUARTER COLUMNS

With the box-like jig shown below, you can rout flutes in a quarter column blank while it is mounted on the lathe. Cut the parts of the jig from ¾-inch plywood, except for the top, which is made from ¼-inch clear acrylic. The jig should be long and wide enough to support the router and high enough to hold the tool just above the column blank when the jig bottom rests on the lathe bed. Once the top, bottom, and sides are assembled, add two vertical braces to make the jig more rigid. Rest the jig on the lathe bed.

Install a double-bearing piloted fluting bit in your router, drill a bit clearance hole through the jig top, and screw the tool's base plate to the jig. The router should be positioned so the bit will lie alongside the column blank when the jig is used. Next, mark cutting lines for the flutes on the blank, then mount the blank on the lathe. Be sure all tools are unplugged during setup. Adjust the cutting depth on the router so the bit is aligned with the cutting line at the midpoint of the blank. Tighten a handscrew around the lathe drive shaft to keep it from rotating. Clamp stop blocks

to the lathe bed so that all the flutes will be the same length.

To use the jig, butt it against one stop block, turn on the router and push on the side of the jig to feed the bit into the blank. Once the pilots are flush against the stock, slide the jig along the lathe bed until it contacts the other stop block. Keep the pilots pressed against the stock as you rout the flute. Turn off the router, remove the handscrew and rotate the blank by hand to align the next cutting line with the bit, and reinstall the handscrew. Cut the remaining flutes *(below)*.

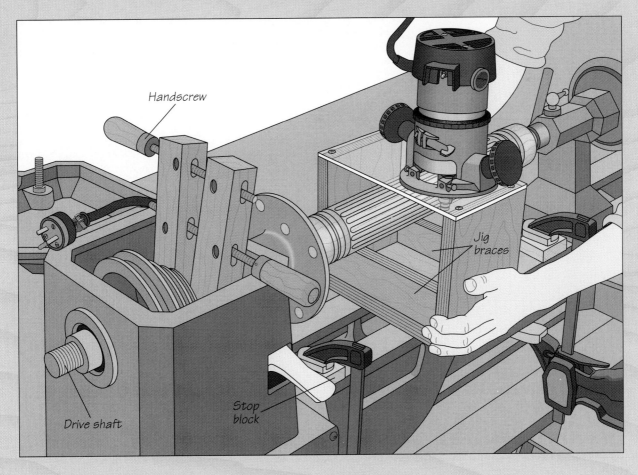

Handscrew

Jig braces

Drive shaft

Stop block

APPLIED SCULPTURES

Scallop shells, stylized sunbursts and fans were popular carvings applied to Queen Anne, Georgian, and Chippendale furniture throughout the 18th Century. Carved by hand, decorative motifs like the one at right were commonly found on the aprons of highboys. They were also used to adorn the knees of cabriole legs and the fronts of central drawers.

A SAMPLING OF FAN AND SHELL MOTIFS

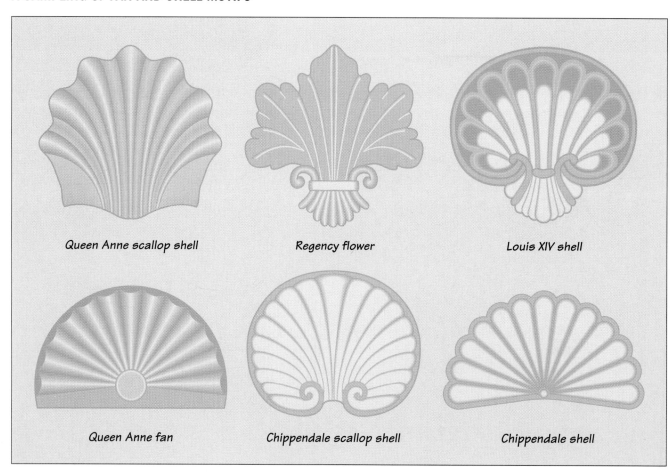

Queen Anne scallop shell   Regency flower   Louis XIV shell

Queen Anne fan   Chippendale scallop shell   Chippendale shell

MAKING AND APPLYING A SCALLOP SHELL

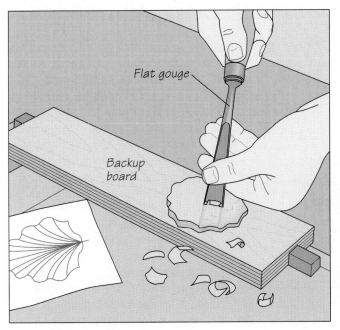

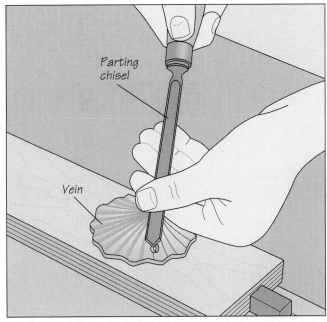

1 Sculpting the shell surface

Draw the shell pattern full-size on a sheet of paper, then transfer your design to a hardwood blank of the desired thickness. Cut the edges of the blank on the band saw and fasten it to a backup board. Secure the backup board to a work surface. Start sculpting the surface of the shell using a flat gouge *(above, left)*, working in the direction of the wood grain. Then transfer the vein lines from your pattern to the blank, and use a parting chisel to etch the lines into the wood *(above, right)*. Cut from the bottom of the blank to the top; to avoid tearout, stop each cut near the top and complete it from the opposite direction.

2 Rounding the rays

Once all the veins have been cut, use the flat gouge to round the contours of the rays between the vein lines. Start by making the surfaces of all the rays convex (or crowning outward). To finish carving the pattern, carve a concave valley into every second ray with a narrow-blade gouge *(left)*. The surfaces of adjacent rays should curve in opposite directions, alternating between convex and concave. Use a parting tool to carve the veins in the wings at the lower sides of the shell *(photo, page 136)*. Once you are satisfied with the shape of the shell, sand the surface lightly. Then detach it from the backup board and glue it in place on the front of the lower chest, using brads to help locate it *(page 123)* and clamps to hold it in place while the adhesive dries.

MAKING AND MOUNTING THE APPLIED MOLDING

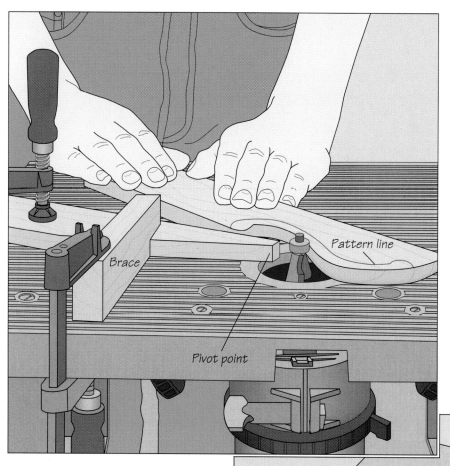

Brace

Pattern line

Pivot point

1 Shaping the volutes on the router table
The curved moldings, called volutes, which decorate the apron of the lower chest, are shaped partially with the router, as shown at left, and partially by hand, as in step 3. Start by making a cardboard template of the molding, then transfer your pattern to a workpiece of the desired thickness. Leave enough waste on the stock to feed it safely across the router table. Cut along one of the pattern lines on the band saw, exposing one edge of the molding. To shape this edge, install a piloted round-over bit in a router and mount the tool in a table. Rather than making the cut freehand, clamp a pivot point to the table in line with the bit, using a brace to steady it. As you feed the workpiece into the bit, brace the stock against the pivot point *(left)*. Make sure you keep the workpiece flush against the bit pilot.

2 Cutting away the remaining waste
Once you have finished shaping one edge of the volute, detach the molding from the waste using the band saw. To keep the blade from binding in the kerf, make a release cut through the waste, stopping at the pattern line. Then saw along the line, feeding the workpiece with both hands *(right)*. Make sure that neither hand is in line with the blade.

Release cut

3 Hand-shaping the second edge

Secure a backup board to a work surface and clamp the molding to the board. Round over the second edge of the volute with a gouge, copying the profile produced by the router bit in step 1 *(right)*. Shape the edge until its contours are smooth; try as much as possible to cut with the grain. Remove the molding from the backup board and sand the surface lightly.

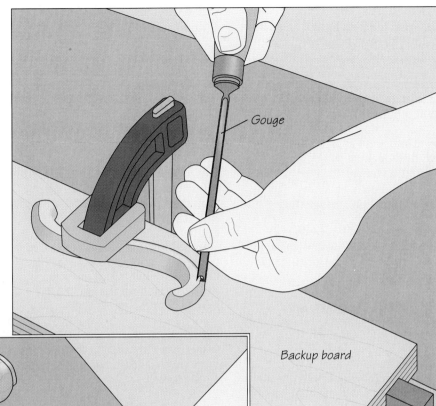

Gouge

Backup board

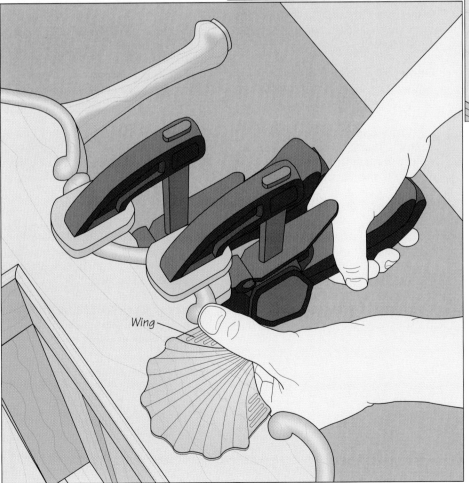

Wing

4 Mounting the volutes

Spread a thin, even layer of glue on the contacting surfaces of the molding and the chest. Clamp the volute in place, lining it up flush with the edge of the bottom rail and leaving a small space between it and the wing of the scallop shell *(left)*. Use two clamps for each piece of molding.

GLOSSARY

A-B-C

Air-dried lumber: Lumber that has reached its equilibrium moisture content by exposure to unheated air.

Batten: A board fastened across the grain of a flat surface such as a chest lid to minimize warping.

Bevel cut: A cut at an angle from face-to-face along the length or width of a workpiece. See *miter cut.*

Biscuit joint: See plate joint.

Board foot: A unit of wood volume measurement equivalent to a piece of wood 1 inch thick and 12 inches square.

Bound water: Moisture present in the cell walls of wood. It remains even after drying; see *free* water.

Cabriole leg: A style of furniture leg characterized by rounded contours designed to imitate the hind leg of a leaping animal.

Carcase: The box-like foundation of a piece of furniture; made from solid panels.

Cockbeading: Narrow projecting molding surrounding the inside edge of a drawer opening.

Cope-and-stick joint: A method of joining stiles and rails in frame-and-panel construction. Tongues in the rails mesh with grooves in the stiles; a decorative molding is cut along the inside edge of the frame.

Cornice or crown molding: Molding attached to the top of a piece of furniture; typically mounted above eye level and angled outwards at 45°.

Crosscut: A cut made across the grain of a workpiece.

Cutting list: A list of the dimensions of the lumber needed for a specific project.

D-E-F

Dado: A rectangular channel cut into a workpiece.

Dentil molding: A decorative detail consisting of a row of small, evenly spaced bars or teeth; usually added to cornice molding.

Dovetail joint: A method of joinery using interlocking pins and tails; the name derives from the distinctive shape cut into the ends of the joining boards.

Dowel center: A metal cylinder that is inserted into a dowel hole to pinpoint a matching hole in a mating workpiece.

Drawer slide: A strip of wood or a commercial metal device fixed to a carcase to support a drawer.

Dust frame: A frame-and-panel assembly installed at the bottom of a piece of furniture or between the drawers to prevent dust from entering.

Edge gluing: Bonding boards together edge-to-edge to form a panel.

Equilibrium moisture content: The moisture content that wood eventually reaches when it is exposed to a given level of relative humidity and temperature.

Escutcheon: A decorative fitting installed around a keyhole to prevent damage to the surrounding wood by the key.

Face frame: A decorative frame attached to the front of a carcase-based bookcase, cabinet, or armoire; also serves to stiffen the structure.

False front: A piece of veneer or wood fixed to the front of a drawer, usually to conceal its joinery.

Fiber saturation point: A condition in which wood cell cavities are free of all water, while the cell walls remain fully saturated.

Finial: An ornament—usually turned and carved—projecting from the upper corners of a furniture piece such as a highboy.

Frame-and-panel joinery: A method of assembling doors and cabinet sides using frames enclosing panels that float in grooves to accommodate shrinkage and swelling of the wood.

Free water: Moisture present in the cell cavities of wood, so called because it is free to evaporate during the drying process; see *bound water.*

G-H-I-J-K

Headstock: The shaft attached to the motor of a lathe; holds work for spindle-turning in conjunction with the tailstock or for turning with a faceplate. See *tailstock.*

Highboy: An elegant 18th Century style of dresser, consisting of an upper and lower chest.